Susanne Lakin was born and brought up in Norfolk and graduated in chemistry from the University of Birmingham. She trained as a chemistry teacher and was Head of Science at The Grange School in Bradford for a number of years and then an Advisory Teacher in Secondary Science. She has completed a PhD in psychology and is the author of a number of education books including revision guides for GCSE and A-level Chemistry, and *Essential Science* for GCSE (Nelson, 1998).

ATOMS IN ACTION

Adventures with....

       Sydney Sodium

Nellie Nitrogen

       Charlie Carbon

Sir Marcus Mercury

Susanne Lakin

The Book Guild Ltd
Sussex, England

First published in Great Britain in 2003 by
The Book Guild Ltd
25 High Street
Lewes, Sussex
BN7 2LU

Copyright © Susanne Lakin 2003

The right of Susanne Lakin to be identified as the author of this work has been asserted by her in accordance with the Copyright, Designs and Patents Act 1988.

All rights reserved. No part of this publication may be reproduced, transmitted, or stored in a retrieval system, in any form or by any means, without permission in writing from the publisher, nor be otherwise circulated in any form of binding or cover other than that in which it is published and without a similar condition being imposed on the subsequent purchaser.

Typesetting in Palatino by
Keyboard Services, Luton, Bedfordshire

Printed in Great Britain by
Athenaeum Press Ltd, Gateshead

A catalogue record for this book is available from
The British Library

ISBN 1 85776 713 6

Contents

Sydney Sodium   1

Nellie Nitrogen   31

Charlie Carbon   57

Sir Marcus Mercury   85

Sydney Sodium

Sydney Sodium was bored.

He stood up, stretched his arms, jostled his electrons and hopped from foot to foot. He had so much energy he didn't know what to do with himself and found it impossible to stay still for long. But he couldn't move far – there just wasn't room. He shrugged his shoulders, tossed his head from side to side and yelled with frustration!

"Owhh! Just let me out of here! I'm so fed up – I just want to get out. It's not fair!"

Sydney Sodium was trapped under a layer of sticky oil in the bottom of a jar on a laboratory shelf. During the years he had seen countless children come and go, lifting other jars off the shelf and carrying out all sorts of exciting experiments.

But his jar was never touched.

The layer of dust on its lid grew steadily thicker and thicker, and the oil above him more smelly and treacly. He was waiting, always waiting, for something to happen. He felt trapped.

"It's not fair," he repeated, stamping his feet. "Let me out!"

But there was no reply.

"It's time I was taken out!"

He thrashed his arms angrily around in the treacly oil but it was so thick that only a tiny ripple formed on its surface.

Suddenly, as if in answer to his outburst, he found himself sliding across the bottom of the jar from side to side. He had been so engrossed in his yelling and thrashing about that he hadn't noticed that a huge hand had grabbed his jar and taken it off the laboratory shelf.

Sydney Sodium could hardly contain himself. He was so excited.

WOW! something was about to happen after all these years.

The oil slurped and sloshed about as he slid backwards and forwards. He could hardly believe it! His jar was actually being lifted from the shelf!

YIPPEE!

Sydney jumped about with excitement, his outermost electron bounced up and down and his neutrons and protons vibrated in anticipation. His jar was carefully placed on a bench and the lid removed. Sydney couldn't see much through the cloud of dust but felt himself being lifted out carefully with a pair of tweezers. For a few seconds he was suspended in mid-air, high above a trough of water standing on the bench.

What was going to happen next?

Suddenly the tweezers opened, and Sydney Sodium fell rapidly through the air, landing with a loud PLOP in the trough of water. He immediately bounced back up to the surface.

"Great!" he shouted. "Freedom at last. Wow! Yippeeeeeee."

His words trailed out behind him as he sped like a torpedo round the trough on the surface of the water. He had no problems staying afloat as, unlike other metals, he was so light that he just couldn't sink even if he had wanted to. The water sprayed up about him as he dashed madly around. When he hit the sides of the trough, he bounced back in again with a bang. It was such fun!

"Wow, this is better than skating. Yippee! Watch out, I'm coming!"

The dashing about was such hot work that he quickly softened and melted into a gleaming silver ball. He felt so good and was very pleased with himself.

Life wasn't so bad after all.

"Hey, who's that?" demanded a shrill voice. It was immediately followed by another, even shriller voice. "What's going on? Stop hitting us."

The two voices continued to direct small explosive questions at Sydney, one after the other, like a stream of electrons. "What are you doing? Can't you stop for a moment? Who are you? Why are you here?"

"Sorrrrry, caaaaan't stooooop!"
Sydney's voice trailed out behind him as he sped past. "I'm moooooving so fast, I caaaan't slow down. It's great fun, you'll haaaaave to keep up with meeee. Coooome on, join in, let's have some fun togetherrrrrrrr."

"But we can't keep up with you. Can't you push us out into the air? Then we could follow."

The two voices belonged to Harry Hydrogen and his sister Hatty. These two atoms were joined together with Olive Oxygen to form a molecule of water. They normally spent their time drifting lazily around in the trough – that is, until Sydney suddenly appeared on the scene.

"Olive isn't bothered but we'd love to come," said Harry.

"OK, watch out as I shoot paaaaast you next time. I'llllll give you a huge puuuuuush!"

As he got near to them, Sydney gave an almighty push and Harry and Hatty popped up out of the water into the air. The force was so great that they began to glow with a yellow flame.

Everywhere Sydney Sodium went, Harry and Hatty Hydrogen followed behind so that he was always surrounded by a bright yellow glow.

Eventually, Sydney Sodium began to run out of energy. He was so exhausted that he came to rest with a short, quiet fizz. At some time during his dashing about he had finally lost his outer electron and changed into an ion. All he could do now was to sink deep into the water.

He sighed with relief.

Life below the surface was quite different. The sounds were muffled and the world was blurred, swaying gently this way and that in wavy lines. Everything was washed in a pale, blue-green hue. It was so peaceful after all that dashing about. Sydney swam slowly around in order to cool off.

"This is the life," he thought. "Better than being stuck under that smelly oil in the jar. But where is everyone?"

With that thought, he suddenly found himself being pushed from behind and forced upwards towards the surface of the water.

"Hey, stop that? What's happening?"

Catherine Chlorine and her twin sister Carlotta were frantically trying to push and pull Sydney out of the water.

"Just stop it!" yelled Sydney. "What d'ya think you're doing?"

"Come on, get out of the water!" yelled Catherine.

"Yeah, you've no right to be here," added her sister. "It's our job to keep it clean."

"Just who do you think you are?" asked Sydney, hanging onto a nearby water molecule and kicking out furiously at the sisters in order to free himself from their clutches.

"I've as much right to be here as you have. I'm not a germ or a bug you know. You'd better concentrate on getting rid of them. After all, that's what you're supposed to do, isn't it?"

"Oops!" Carlotta looked slightly embarrassed. "Sssorry, I never realised – we just get carried way with chasing the germs and thought you were one."

"Yeah," confirmed Catherine. She stopped and then stared at Sydney, looking him up and down. "So, we've someone new to join us. Ummm! Not bad." She winked at Carlotta. "We could have some fun together. How about a game of catch the ion?"

Carlotta looked disapprovingly at her sister.

"You can play if you want, but I've got work to do." With that she swam off and disappeared.

Before long, shouts of "Got you!", "No you haven't!", "Let me go, you're hurting!" and "Come on, can't catch me!" echoed around and around the trough.

Sydney and Catherine were so engrossed in their game that they didn't notice that their trough of water had been tipped into the sink. The game continued as the water rushed down the drain and along the sewers, through the treatment plants, into the river and finally out to sea.

They carried on playing their games year after year.

The sun shone, the winters came, the winds blew and the clouds broke, but Sydney and Catherine continued to play. Under the sea there were plenty of hiding places among the weeds, corals and anemones – life was fun.

But one particular year the summer was extra long and hot. The sun shone relentlessly and heated up the sea. Many of the water molecules gained so much energy that they bounced out through the surface and escaped into the air where they formed new cotton-wool clouds. The volume of water around Sydney and Catherine decreased. It became hot – too hot for games. In fact, too hot for doing much at all. Soon there was hardly any room for them to move around as more and more of the water evaporated.

Catherine clung to Sydney in despair.

"Oh, what are we going to do?" she muttered. "The sun is drying up the sea. There's hardly any water left."

Sydney also felt dejected. Something about their situation reminded him of his former life in his jar, but at least there was no smelly oil!

He put his arm around Catherine and reassured her. "Never mind. We've got each other – we're not on our own."

"Oooh Sydney," exclaimed Catherine, "I'm so glad you're here. It would be awful without you."

"Umm, I'm glad, too," murmured Sydney, but he was not quite so sure that this was how he wanted to spend the rest of his life. He was beginning to feel trapped again, and wanted to escape.

As the sea evaporated, Sydney and Catherine grew closer together, attracted to each other like the north and south poles of a magnet. The force between them was so overwhelming that there was no way Sydney could resist. They were no longer separate and able to play together as friends around the ocean. Instead, they had become a pair, stuck together to form a small crystal of salt.

Together they made an important chemical compound, a compound called sodium chloride.

"Phew," muttered Sydney one bright sunny day. "It's so hot, I can't bear it any longer."

He wiped the perspiration off his brow with the back of his hand and looked round.

"Hey, Catherine!" he exclaimed with surprise. "Just look what's happened! We're on dry land!"

The water around them had evaporated completely and in its place had left piles of shiny, white, glistening crystals. The sun reflected off their flat surfaces producing a dazzling spectacle. Sydney and Catherine found themselves sitting close together on the top of one of the highest crystals, looking down at the wonderland around.

'Oooh," murmured Catherine, "this is so beautiful. I could never have imagined anything quite like this!"

Many days passed with Sydney and Catherine marooned on top of their gleaming white crystal. Sometimes, at high tide, more sea water surrounded them, but it quickly evaporated leaving yet more crystals behind. At first it was amazing to watch the wilderness of white crystals grow, but after a while Sydney became bored and frustrated again.

"Oh, I wish I could move," he said, trying to free himself from Catherine's clutches.

"Careful, you're hurting," complained Catherine. "Just watch what you're doing!"

But Sydney didn't care, and began to pull and push. "I just want to be free!"

He stomped his feet and thrashed his arms about as much as he could but it made no difference. They were stuck together and there was nothing he could do about it.

"Just calm down," said Catherine. "Be patient. Something will happen, you'll see."

"I'm fed up," snapped Sydney. "I need to *move*, I need some *space* of my *own*."

"There's nothing you can do about it," retorted Catherine. "Don't be so childish!"

As you can imagine their quarrel developed. Catherine and Sydney were so busy arguing that it came as quite a shock to suddenly feel their mountain of salt begin to move.

Things were happening quickly.

Their pile of crystals was scooped up and tipped into a railway wagon and carried off, away from the hot, white wilderness. Life became exciting again as the train raced through the countryside past fields, forests, farms and houses, all at a tremendous speed.

Finally, after several exhausting hours, Catherine and Sydney found themselves at the top of yet another pile of salt in a large factory.

But their journey didn't end there.

Before long they were scooped up again and dropped into a huge container where they sat huddled together wondering what was going to happen next. The temperature soared and Sydney and Catherine gained more energy.

"Look at me!" shouted Catherine, "I can begin to move."

"So can I!" replied Sydney with relief.

They jostled furiously backwards and forwards and from side to side, gradually overcoming the sticky forces which held them together. Their movements became more frantic, until suddenly – **PING** – Sydney and Catherine broke free from each other. The salt had melted and they swam around in the hot liquid. It was even more fun than being in the sea. They had so much energy they could swim even faster.

"At last, freedom!" yelled Sydney as he sped past.

"Can't catch me!" teased Catherine as she swam off in the opposite direction.

At that instant, Sydney suddenly felt a strange tingling sensation which pulled him across to one side of the huge container.

An electric current had been switched on. He couldn't stop! He sped even faster.

The force was so great that he felt his electrons would be stripped from his skin. So he concentrated hard on keeping himself together and just had time to yell "Bye!" as Catherine sped past him in the opposite direction.

"Bye, bye!" she yelled back. "Take care! It's been fun, hasn't it?"

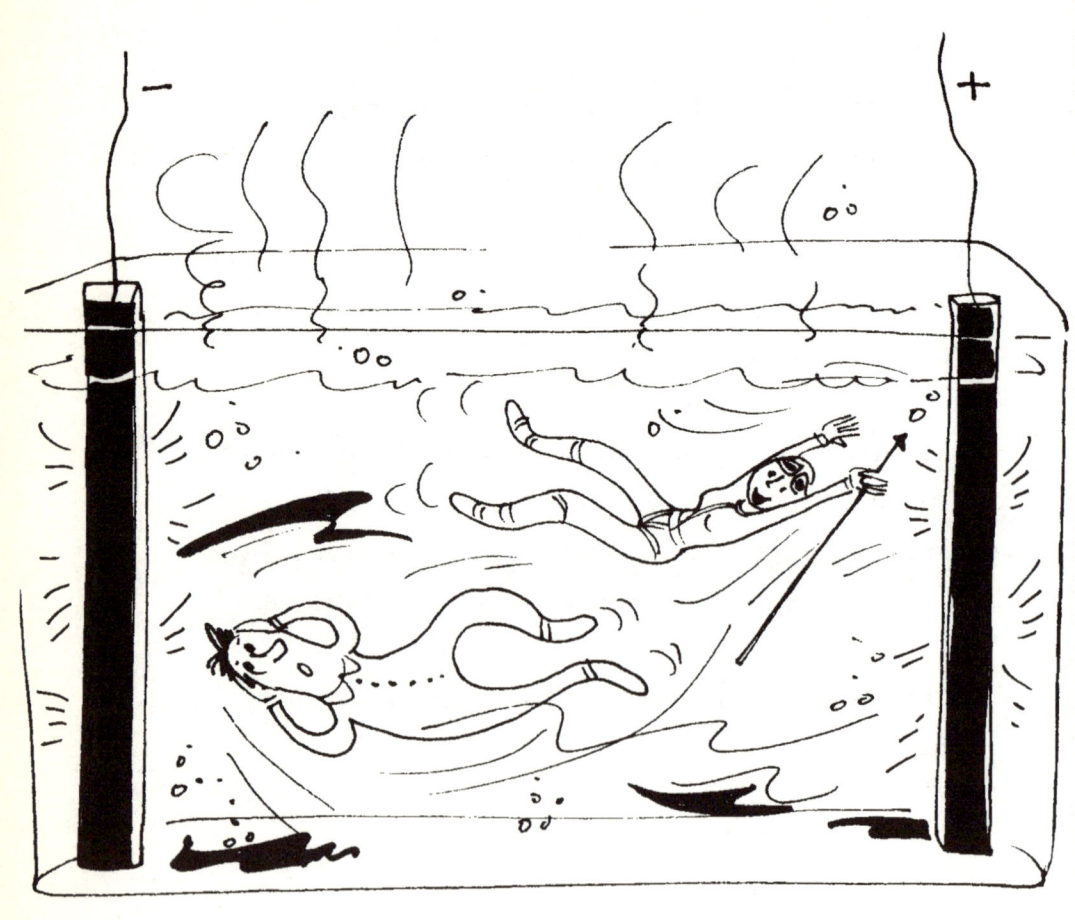

A huge iron electrode suddenly loomed up in front of Sydney Sodium and he buried his head in his hands as he sped towards it.

"Oh, no!" he said, too frightened to look.

BANG!

He hit the surface with an almighty force which jostled his electrons, protons and neutrons so much that he was dazed. After a few minutes he carefully opened his eyes and saw that an electron had jumped back into his shell so that he was no longer an ion. He was an atom again and found himself bouncing out of the liquid up to its surface as a tiny, shiny, metal sphere once more.

"Great!" he muttered. "I'm me again! At last!"

Floating up to the surface, he jumped up and down feeling whole and happy with himself – an atom of sodium once again.

But Sydney didn't stay by the metal electrode for long. It was much too hot, so he quickly made his excuses and left.

Eventually, a few days later, he noticed a job for sodium atoms advertised in a local shop window.

> **WANTED: SODIUM ATOMS**
> **Must be prepared to work night shifts.**
> **Good money.**

"Just the thing," he though. "Time to try something different. Stops me getting bored."

Within a few days after getting the job, Sydney Sodium found himself in a large, glass tube held high above a busy street in a small village. Life was exciting once again.

During the day, Sydney Sodium peered down into the street and watched the antics of the humans rushing by in their cars and dashing backwards and forwards and in and out of the shops. He began to learn a lot about them from the way they looked and walked, who they spoke to and what they said. It was fascinating. What a strange group of beings!

Very few of them ever looked up to see him staring down, or even had time to admire the clouds or sky. They were all intent on getting on with their busy lives.

At night, Sydney's job began.

As the sun set, an electric current was switched on and Sydney felt a wonderful, tingling sensation throughout the whole of his body. It was so exciting that his outer electron would bounce up and down until suddenly it had enough energy to jump away into the space above. A few seconds later it would return and give out the energy as a bright yellow flash of light. Sydney would feel a wonderful surge of pride as the street below became bathed in his golden haze, *his own golden haze*, which came from *him*. And all this excitement occurred in a fraction of a second, and was repeated time and time again throughout the long night, until dawn crept over the horizon.

What a job! He had no time to ever feel bored!

Perfect.

Sydney could not have hoped for anything better. During the day he could get rid of his excess energy by doing a few cartwheels up and down the length of his tube. There was plenty of room for exercising.

So there he is, high above the street, giving off his yellow glow, night after night.

Next time it's dark, just glance up at a street light and see if you can make out Sydney Sodium sitting there, glowing with pride. He'll be there, just you see, working away, as busy as ever.

SODIUM

- Sodium is a soft, silvery metal which is so reactive that it is kept in oil.

- When a small piece of sodium is dropped into water it fizzes, melts and moves rapidly around on the surface.
  It reacts with the water to give off hydrogen.
  The hydrogen burns and the sodium colours the flame yellow.
  The sodium decreases in size as each sodium atom loses an electron, to form a sodium ion which dissolves in the water. Sodium hydroxide solution is left:

  sodium + water —> sodium hydroxide + hydrogen

- Sodium forms many ionic compounds. The most common is sodium chloride, or salt.
  Sodium chloride is a white, crystalline solid which dissolves in water.
  Some sodium chloride is obtained from sea water by evaporation using the heat of the sun.

- Solid crystalline sodium chloride melts at a high temperature. When an electric current is passed through the melted sodium chloride, metallic sodium is obtained at the negative electrode or cathode. Chlorine gas is obtained at the positive electrode or anode.

- When an electric current is passed through a tube containing sodium vapour at a low pressure, a yellow light is given out.
  This is because the outer electron around the sodium atom takes in energy and moves further from the centre or nucleus. When it returns to its original position, the energy is given out as yellow light.

Nellie Nitrogen

"PHEW!"

Nellie Nitrogen sighed.

"PHEW," she sighed again. "It's **SO** hot!"

Beads of perspiration trickled down her forehead. Nellie fumbled with the clasp of her handbag and brought out a delicate lace handkerchief smelling of lavender and mothballs. She mopped her brow, undid her silk scarf and removed her gloves.

"Oh, that's better, but I'm still too hot."

Carefully, she took off her blue felt hat with its pink feather and placed it on the ground beside her. Nellie was **never** seen without a hat, so it must have been very hot indeed. Her grey-white hair formed damp curls around her face and her silk blouse stuck to her skin.

"Perhaps I'm ill. Maybe I've got a temperature, I do feel strange, a bit dizzy – but where am I?"

Nellie Nitrogen peered around but everything was hazy and shrouded in a soft, fine mist.

"Perhaps it's my eyes. I'll have to have them tested. Oh dear, I must be getting old!"

The air felt heavy and all was quiet except for a faint rustling noise, the drone of insects and a steady drip, drip, drip.

"What's that noise? Not my ears as well!"

Drip, drip, drip.

"Maybe I'm in a steamy bathroom – but there aren't any towels or taps." She peered again. "Only plants, loads of them, I can just make them out. But where am I, what's happened to me?"

Nellie screwed up her eyes and the huge green leaf of a rubber plant came into focus, surrounded by other leaves and exotic flowers. A drop of water collected on the edge of the leaf and grew larger and larger till, finally, it fell off with a plop. Other drops fell from branches, flowers and creepers. The air was heavy with their sickly perfume.

All of a sudden, the steady drone of the insects was punctuated by the harsh screech of a parrot.

"Gosh, I must be in a forest! But however did I get here? Whatever's happened?"

Nellie leaned against the side of a large yellow banana and closed her eyes, trying to remember what had happened that morning.

It was Wednesday, and Wednesday was her day for playing Atomic Bridge with Leopold Lead, Naomi Neon and Felicity Phosphorus. After her usual breakfast of fruit juice, coffee, wholemeal toast and homemade marmalade, she had left the house. She remembered closing the gate and walking down the road, but after that everything was hazy. The traffic fumes had been thick and the air was still and humid. She remembered sitting on the bench at the bus stop and then ... nothing.

A blank.

Try as she might, she couldn't remember anything else at all.

"Hi, Nellie Nitrogen, you all right?"

Nellie nearly jumped out of her electrons, almost squashing her hat as she landed.
"What happened to you this morning?"

Olive Oxygen was hovering nearby, bouncing about, as full of energy as ever.
"Oh, it's you, Olive. Where have you come from? I'm a bit dizzy – I don't know where I am."
"Everyone was worried when you didn't turn up for bridge. Naomi sent me out to look, and here you are!"

She paused and took Nellie's hand. "You OK? You look a bit dazed."
"Erm, yes, er, that is, er, no, not really. Maybe I need one of my pills. Perhaps my protons are playing up. I feel a bit strange. I don't know what's happened – it's so hot and humid."
"Oh, don't worry, you'll be OK – I'm here now." Olive patted her hand reassuringly.

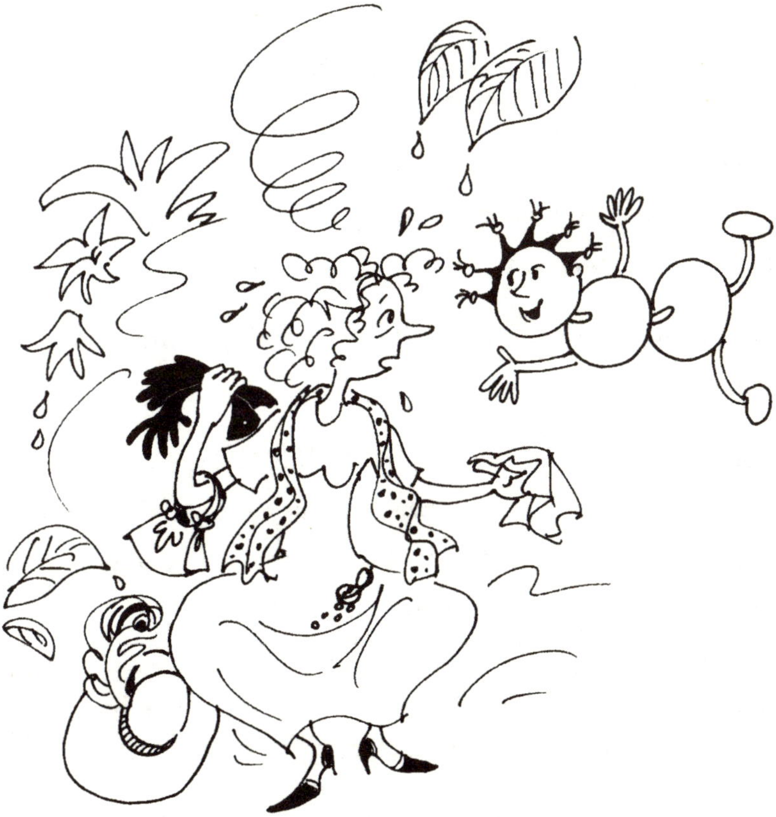

Nellie fumbled in her bag and brought out a tiny, red box.

"Let's see: pink pills for protons, navy for neutrons ... or is it the purple for protons? Oh dear, I can't remember..." her words trailed off.

"Put those away and just relax, everything's fine," said Olive.

"But where are we?" continued Nellie. "All these plants and flowers. Are we in a forest? Have I missed the game – oh, what will they all think of me? I never miss a game! Ooh, I'm so sorry, I'm getting quite forgetful."

She mopped her eyes with her fine lace handkerchief smelling of lavender and mothballs.

"Just stop worrying," said Olive calmly. "We're in the hothouse in the park at the end of your road, so you haven't wandered far. You were probably blown here by the wind. It sometimes happens to me, too. We're both so light that with one large gust of wind we can be off."

She continued reassuringly, "It's not surprising you feel dizzy. It's so hot and clammy today, even worse in this greenhouse, and the traffic fumes are terrible. You're probably hungry, that's all – here, have a crisp. I always carry some in case I get peckish."

Olive opened up a packet of protonic Pringles.

Just as Nellie was about to bite into the crisp, there was a brilliant flash of light. It sliced through the misty haze and reflected off the shiny leaves of the plants. For a second, the world sprang into life as a kaleidoscope of brilliant colours. The flash was followed by an almighty ROAR which made the leaves vibrate and showered both atoms with heavy drops of water.

"Ooooh, what was that?" cried Nellie, dropping her crisp and gloves, and then her handbag as she tried to pick them all up.

"Just a storm. A good thing – it'll clear the air, especially if it rains. Come on, let's get outside."

Olive grabbed Nellie as she put on her gloves and hat and made for an open window in the hothouse.

Outside things were really happening. Nellie shivered at the sudden drop in temperature and clung to Olive. The sky was dark with angry clouds and the trees creaked and groaned in the wind.

SSSSWWWWIIISH!

Nellie grabbed frantically at her hat as the wind snatched it and ripped off the pink feather. "Oh, my best hat ruined," she sobbed as the feather disappeared out of sight.

BANG! CRASH!

Nellie almost jumped out of her electrons as the hothouse door slammed shut and a pane of glass smashed on the ground.

"Eeeeee, this is fun! What a storm – it's super!" yelled Olive into Nellie's ear. But her words were lost as the wind screeched through the creepers and plants in the hothouse, tearing their leaves to shreds.

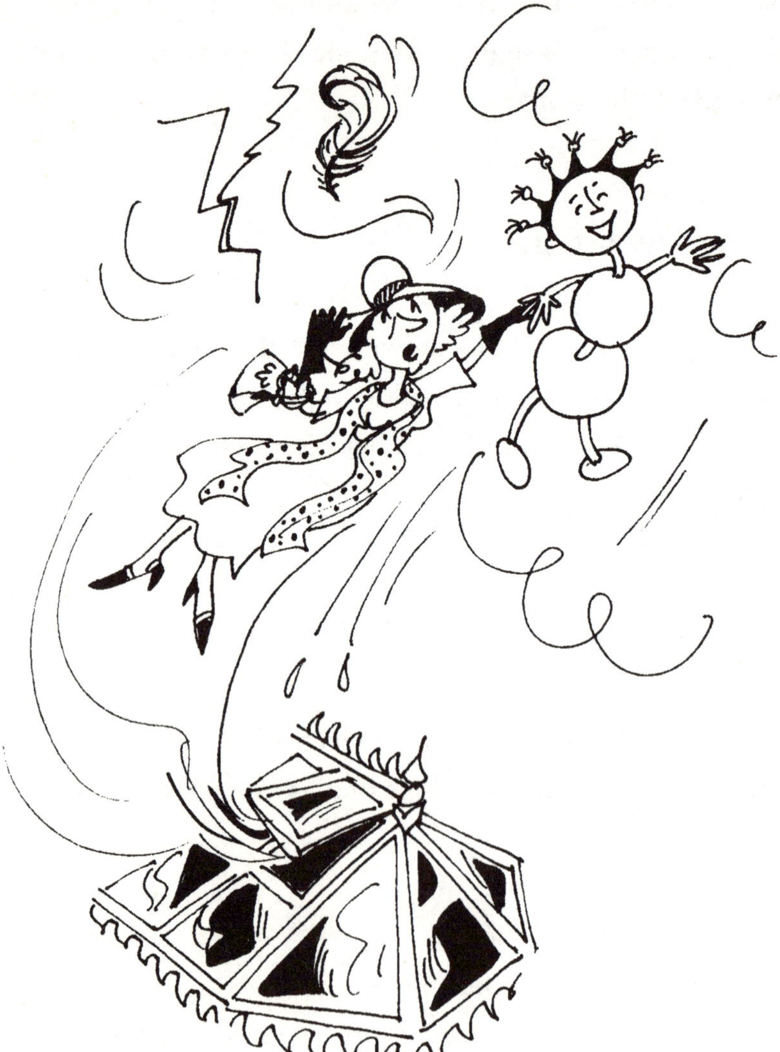

CRACKLE!

The sky was lit up from horizon to horizon by a brilliant streak of lightning coming from a jagged gap between the huge black clouds. The clouds smashed together and there was a deafening roar.

"Come on!" yelled Olive. "This is exciting. Let's get closer."

"Oh, no!" protested Nellie, "I'm frightened."

But her words were drowned by another CRASH and she was dragged off behind Olive, frantically clinging to her hand.

Up, up, up, up they went, deep into the darkest depths of the clouds.

"Oh dear," sighed Nellie, "we'll never survive. It's terrifying!"

The clouds closed in around them. Huge drops of water sped past on their way to earth and molecules and atoms smashed together in the swirling currents of air.

Olive pulled Nellie backwards and forwards to avoid collisions, laughing excitedly as she yelled, "Yippee, this is as good as being on the dodgems!"

Nellie closed her eyes and clung grimly to Olive's hand. She had never been so frightened in all her life. The atmosphere was electric and her hair stood on end.

"Oh, my perm – what will I do? It'll never..."

There was a brilliant flash and the end of her sentence was drowned with an almighty **SMASH, CRASH, BOOOOOM!**

Nellie was sure that she was having one of her electron attacks.

"Where are my pills? Oh, now what do I take for my electrons? The egg-shaped ones or the enormous ones? I can't remember. Ohhhh help me! What's happening to my electrons? Ohhhh!"

Something peculiar had definitely happened. Some of Nellie's electrons had been pulled towards Olive, and, in turn, some of Olive's electrons had been pulled towards Nellie. The atoms were fastened tightly together – so tightly, in fact, that they were unable to shake themselves free.

"What's happened to us?" asked Nellie, feeling very frightened.

"I think," replied Olive slowly, "we've joined together to become a molecule."

"How's that? What kind of molecule?" Nellie hated change – nothing would ever be the same again.

"Well," said Olive wisely, "you're an atom of nitrogen and I'm an atom of oxygen, so together we must have formed a molecule of nitrogen oxide. Hey, that's fun! It must have happened during that huge flash of light..."

But her words were drowned by another almighty **BOOOOOM** that shook the sky. The shockwave sent our friends hurtling down towards earth at a tremendous speed.

SPLASH!
A huge drop of rain sloshed over them and, struggling inside, they were carried faster and faster, ever downwards.

PLOP!
They landed with a dull thud on the ground by the side of an ancient oak tree.

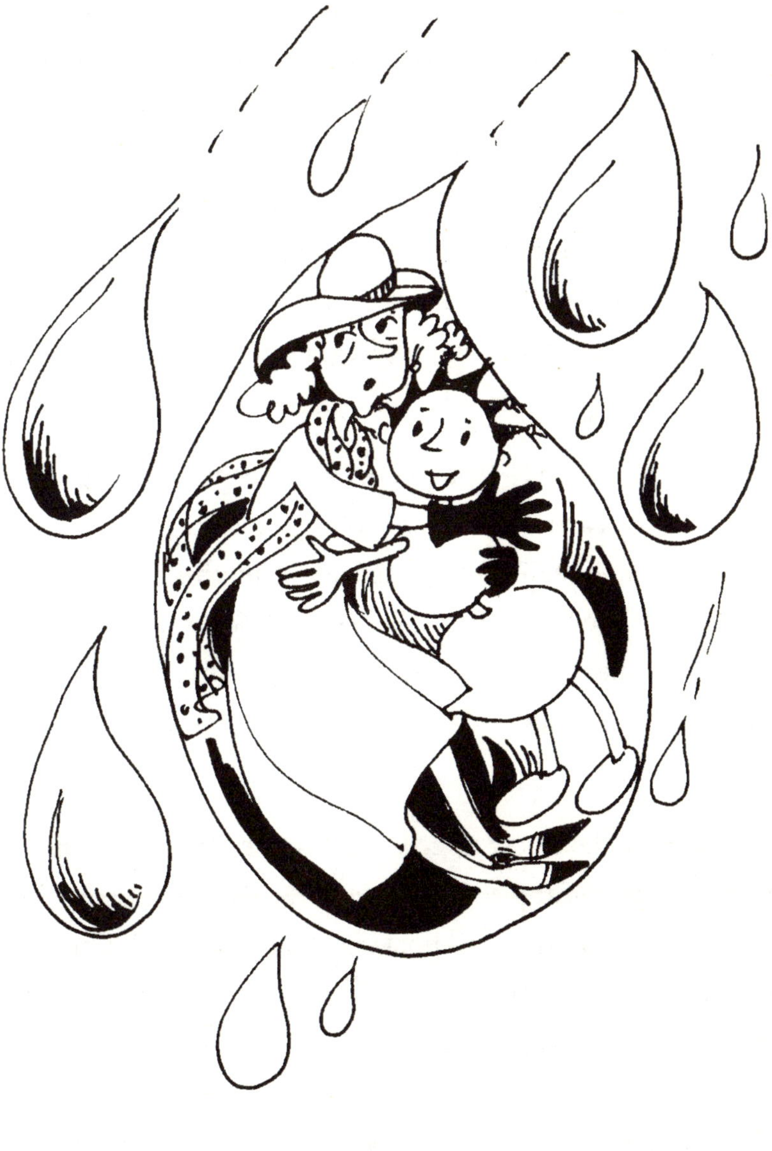

Olive and Nellie struggled in the water but it was impossible to escape. More drops fell, then even more, and they found themselves sinking deeper and deeper into the soil. It grew steadily darker and colder. Both Nellie and Olive were glad of each other's company.

"Oh dear, do you think we'll ever escape back into the air again?" sobbed Nellie. "I'll never complain about my aches and pains, if only we could get out of here."

But they continued to sink deeper and deeper into the bowels of the earth. There was no hope of escape. Gradually, they realised that instead of moving downwards they were being sucked sideways. At first the suction was hardly noticeable, but after a while it grew stronger and stronger.

They were sucked past huge jagged rocks, through pools of water, round lumps of coal, along the sides of slimy worms and through small pockets of air in the soil. On and on, until finally they came face to face with the entrance to a huge hole – the gaping mouth of a dark, endless tunnel.

"Here we go," yelled Olive. "Hang onto your handbag!"

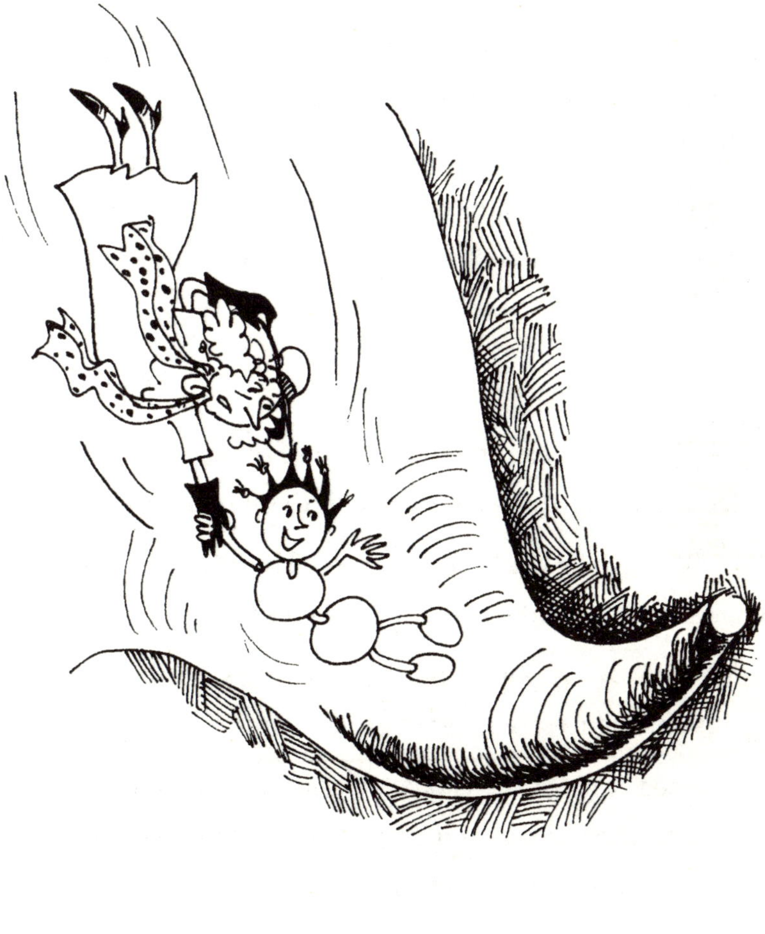

WHOOOOSH!

They were sucked at a tremendous speed into the tunnel and along its length.

"Hey, this is fun!" yelled Olive.

"I don't think so," retorted Nellie, her ears popping as they were sucked upwards. "Where are we? It's frightening."

"Oh just relax and enjoy yourself," said Olive. "I think we're inside the roots of that huge oak tree and being sucked up into its trunk. Oooops, sorry!"

Olive apologised as they bumped into other atoms and molecules being sucked along with them in the tunnel.

"Hey, it's Charlie Carbon and Harry Hydrogen isn't it? What are you two doing here?" asked Olive.

"I don't know," replied Charlie, yawning sleepily. "Me, I'm just trying to sleep, that's all. I'm tired."

"We're heading for the leaves," added Harry. "Fun, isn't it? Like an upside-down helter skelter. I think we might all end up there together, don't you?"

"Oh, what do you mean?" asked Nellie frantically.

"Just wait and see," came the reply. "Here we come, hang onto your electrons."

With these words, Nellie and Olive were suddenly blinded by the brilliant light of the sun.

"Oh!" yelled Nellie. "My eyes hurt. What's happening?"

"We're on a leaf," said Charlie Carbon sleepily. "Just be quiet for a bit now, can't you? I'm so tired, I need to get some sleep."

And there they were, sitting on the top of a large green oak leaf in the bright spring sunshine. And what's more, they were all joined together: Charlie Carbon, Harry Hydrogen, Olive Oxygen and Nellie Nitrogen. Together they formed part of the long chain of a huge new molecule – a molecule called a protein which made up part of the leaf.

"You can see how important we are now," said Harry Hydrogen proudly. "This tree couldn't possibly survive without us. We're the substance that helps it to grow."

"Oh, is that so?" replied Nellie, not quite convinced.

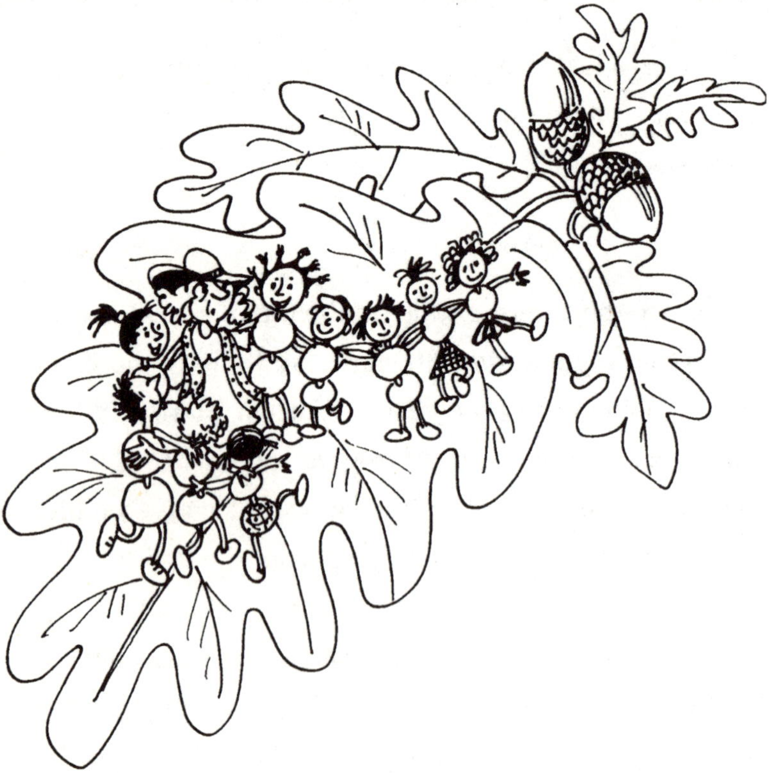

All the same, Nellie felt a lot happier. At least she was out in the open air again and free to look around and see what the other atoms were getting up to. After a short while she dozed off, exhausted by all her adventures. There was no danger of her being blown off the leaf as she was attached firmly to the other atoms in their molecule of protein. So whatever happened to her would also happen to them. Perhaps they'd all begin a game of Atomic Bridge later, you never knew.

Eventually, the days grew shorter, the weather colder and autumn came. The leaves dried up, turned red and brown, shrivelled up and fell to the ground. Nellie was no longer on the top of the oak tree.

Our friends spent the winter buried deep under a pile of leaves, all holding tightly onto each other to keep warm. They slept for most of the time in a state of semi-hibernation. By spring, the leaves had rotted down and were gradually disappearing.

Months later, Nellie woke up to find that Olive Oxygen, Harry Hydrogen and Charlie Carbon had disappeared. She stretched, got up and bounced around, pleased with her unexpected freedom, and found her sister Nora nearby. They chatted non-stop and then wandered off home together to share breakfast – wholemeal toast, homemade marmalade and a steaming mug of creamy fresh coffee.

"Oh," sighed Nellie, "this is what I've missed more than anything! So much has happened, Nora, I'll have to tell you about it. But not now, I'm just so happy to be home."

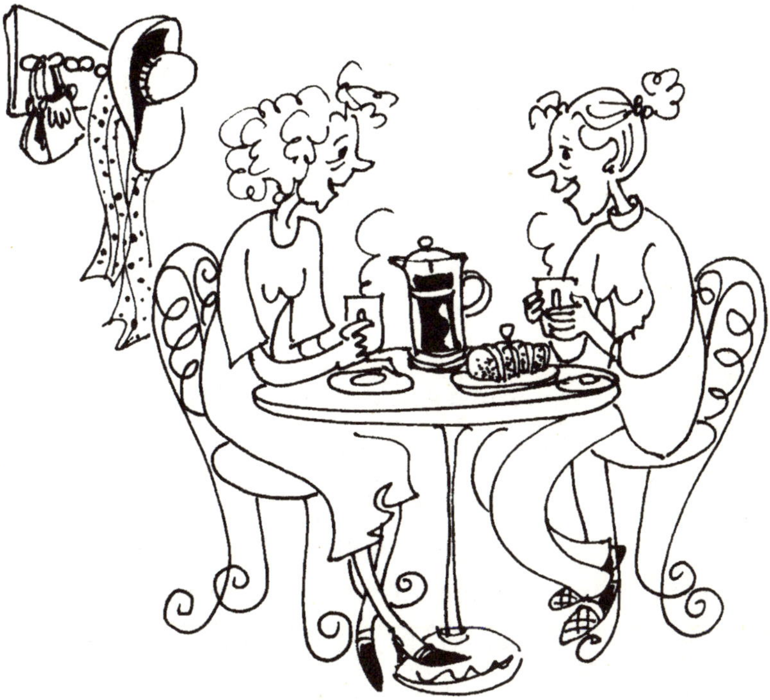

She sighed. "Now I must water my plants, and do a bit of dusting. And then, let's see, it must be Wednesday today – Atomic Bridge day. Perhaps they're all waiting for me. I'll have to go and find out. Now, where's my hat? Oh, here it is, but it seems to have lost its feather. I wonder what's happened to it? Oh well, never mind."

With that, Nellie Nitrogen wandered off, muttering to herself.

She joined the atoms in a game of bridge, just like old times. It was as though all her adventures had never taken place. In fact, she quite forgot about them until she put on her best hat and noticed its missing feather. For a moment she would wonder where she had lost it, but only for a moment. Then she would shrug her shoulders, murmur "Never mind" and get on with whatever she was doing at the time.

NITROGEN

- At room temperature, nitrogen is a colourless, odourless, tasteless gas. It makes up over three-quarters of the air.

- Nitrogen is not a very reactive gas. However, in the presence of lightning, nitrogen and oxygen in the air join together to form the gas called nitrogen oxide. This reacts with more oxygen in the air, dissolves in water and eventually forms nitrates in the soil. These are taken in by plants and used to make proteins. Proteins also contain carbon and hydrogen.

- When plants die their proteins are broken down by bacteria in the soil and nitrogen gas is released into the air.

- This sequence of events forms part of an important cycle called the **NITROGEN CYCLE**.

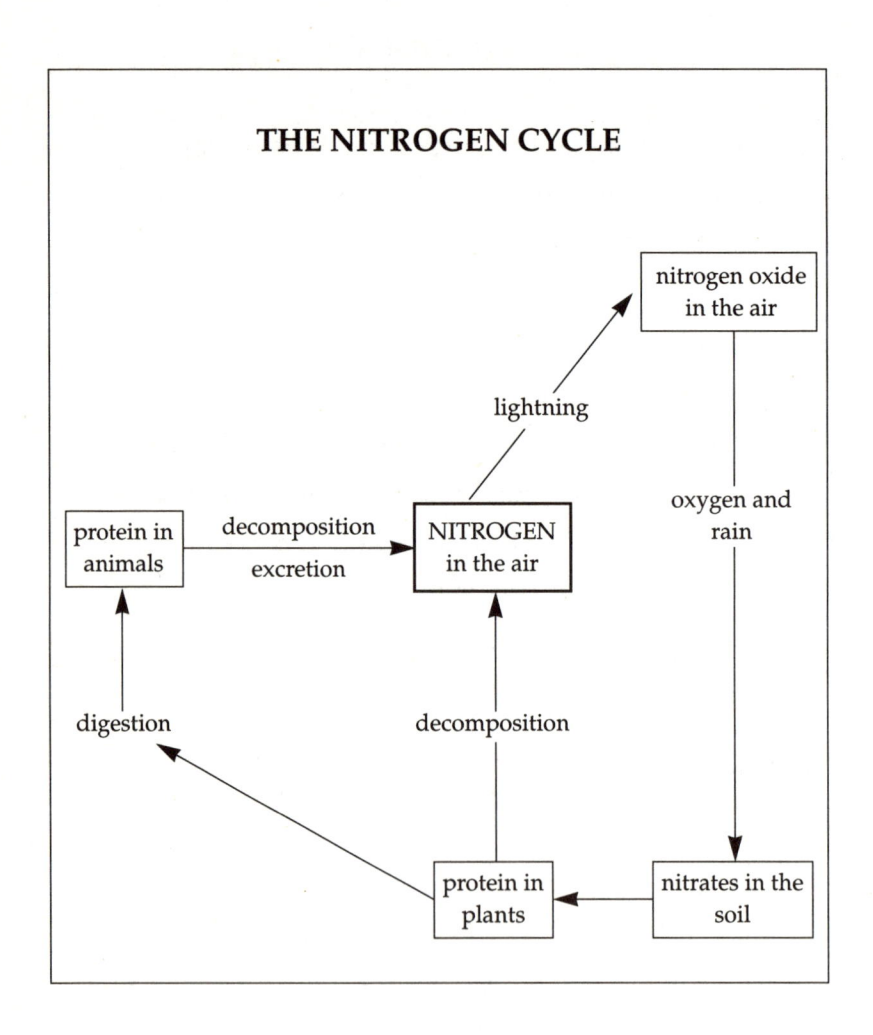

THE NITROGEN CYCLE

- nitrogen oxide in the air
- NITROGEN in the air (via lightning)
- oxygen and rain → nitrates in the soil
- nitrates in the soil → protein in plants
- protein in plants → NITROGEN in the air (decomposition)
- protein in plants → protein in animals (digestion)
- protein in animals → NITROGEN in the air (decomposition, excretion)

Charlie Carbon

Uggggggggh, phewwwwwwww. Uggggggggh, phewwwwwww.

Charlie Carbon is asleep.

Uggggggggh, phewwwwwwww. Uggggggggh, phewwwwwww.

Charlie Carbon is always asleep.

Uggggggggh, phewwwwwwww. Uggggggggh, phewwwwwww.

Gently snoring away, a small wizened figure, curled up in a hollow on a piece of coal buried deep underground.

Uggggggggh, phewwwwwwww. Uggggggggh, phewwwwwww.

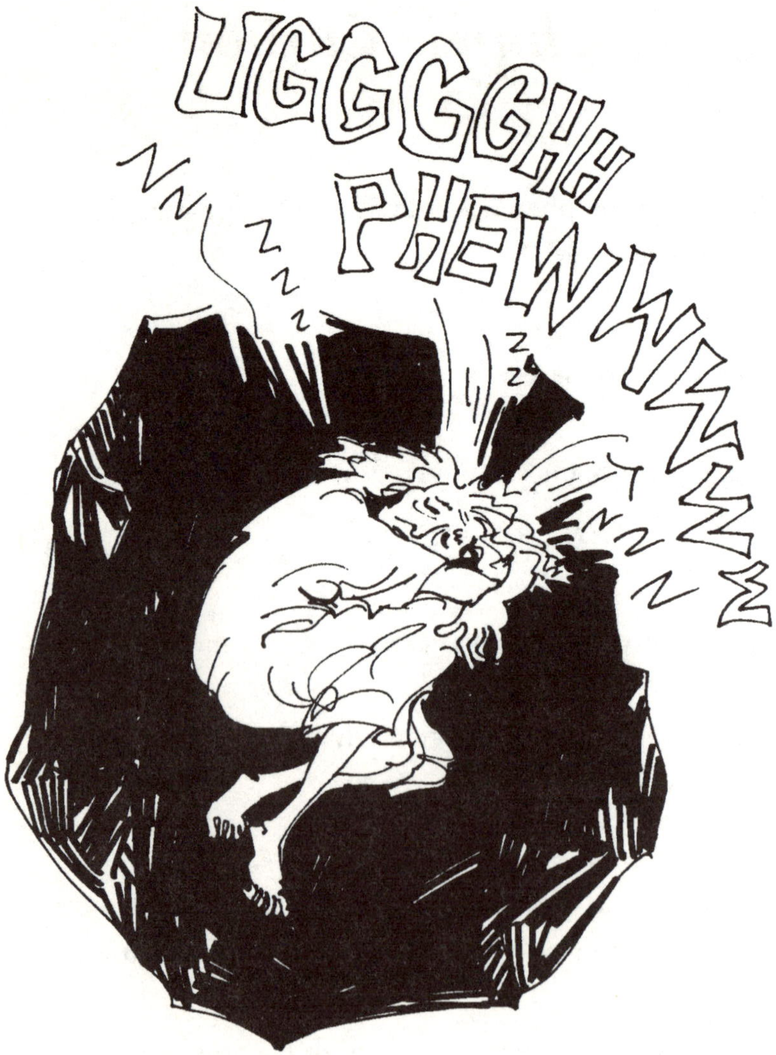
UGGGGHH
PHEWWWWE
ZZZZZ

Sydney Sodium

Nellie Nitrogen

Charlie Carbon

Sir Marcus Mercury

In the dim light, you can just make out a thin, old lady with grey frizzy hair and a face lined with a thousand wrinkles. Her small sunken eyes are almost hidden under bushy eyebrows covered by a layer of coal dust. Every time Charlie Carbon breathes out, tiny particles of dust dance around her nose and settle back on her face again as she breathes in.

But how long had she been there? No one knows. Even Charlotte Carbon, or Charlie as everyone calls her, doesn't remember. Perhaps a thousand years, maybe a hundred thousand or over a million – she has no idea. All she knows is that she wants to sleep, to be left alone, peaceful and warm, curled up on the shiny black coal.

Charlie Carbon continues to snore, day after day, week after week, year after year.

Uggggggggh, phewwwwwwwww. Uggggggggh, phewwwwwwwww.

BANG! THUD!!! CRASH!!!!!

The peace is shattered in a second. Charlie Carbon wakes up with a jolt and sits up sharply, banging her head on another piece of coal.

"Ow! What's that? Ohhhh!" The earth shakes violently and throws her against a piece of coal jutting out by her side. "Stop it, whoever you are! You've woken me up!"

There is another bang and a piece of coal breaks free and lands on her foot.

"Ow! What's happening? Go away! I want to sleep."

The earth heaves up and down and Charlie Carbon is shaken from side to side. Deafening explosions echo all around her, followed by thuds, screeches, roars and rumbles that cause her teeth to chatter and the bones in her body to vibrate.

Charlie is wide awake and very frightened. She grips tightly onto the lump of coal at her side until her knuckles turn white under their layer of grey coal dust. Nothing like this has ever happened before. Never once, during the many long years she has spent sleeping peacefully, deep in the belly of the earth.

The bangs grow louder and louder and get nearer and nearer until the protons and neutrons in Charlie's brain seem to rattle together. She clings grimly to her rock as it starts to heave and move violently, backwards and forwards, up and down, side to side. As she bounces about she angrily utters loud shrieks every time she is thrown against the hard surface.

"Ouch! Ohhhh! Ough!! Oh, not again! What's happening? I can't stand it. Stop it, now, at once!"

As if in answer to her pleas, the noise and movements suddenly stop. Still clinging to her lump of coal, Charlie finds herself on a smooth rubbery surface. It is moving slowly but steadily upwards, so Charlie is able to relax and loosen her grip.

"Pheeeewwwww!"

She takes out a crumpled grey handkerchief and mops up the beads of perspiration which are trickling down her face. They leave long pale streaks in the grey surface of her skin.

She is exhausted, but her journey is only just beginning!

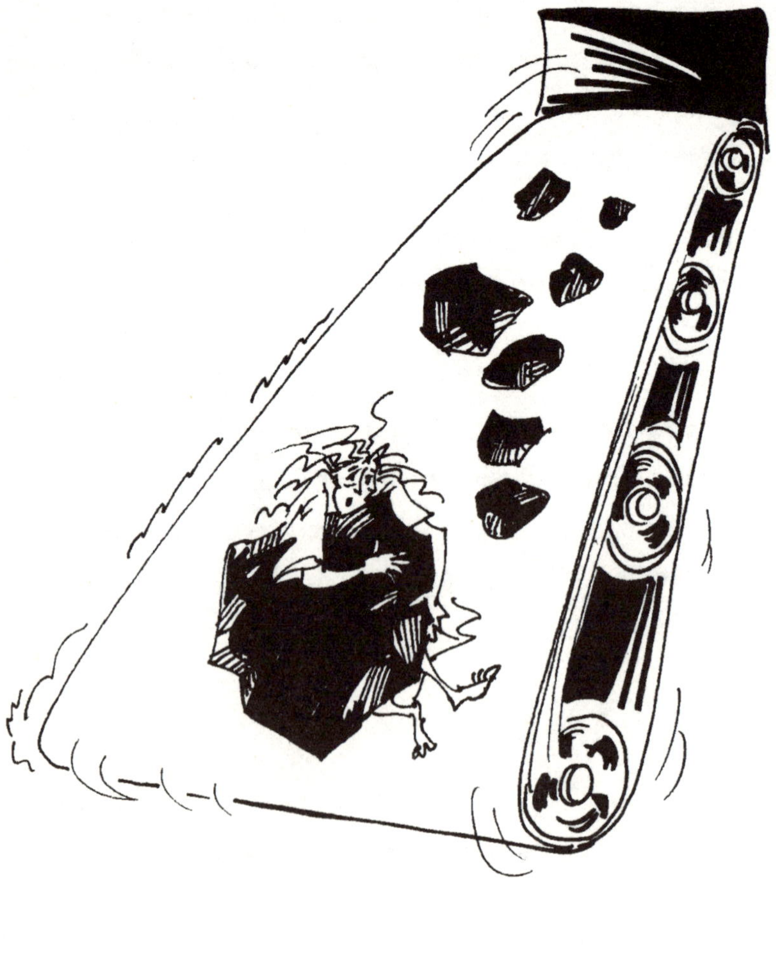

The conveyer belt carrying Charlie Carbon on her piece of coal gathers speed. It moves quickly upwards out of the mine towards the surface of the earth. Charlie's ears pop with the rapid change in pressure. She swallows frantically to relieve the discomfort.

Gradually, however, the rhythmical rocking movements of the belt and the steady whirr of the engines make her feel incredibly tired. Yawning, she relaxes, settles down and curls up in a crevice on the surface of the coal. She is soon fast asleep.

Uggggggggggh, phewwwwwwwww. Uggggggggggh, phewwwwwwww.

Suddenly, she is woken again – this time by a brilliant white light which penetrates her eyelids.

"What's happening now? Not an explosion! I can't stand much more!"

But it is no explosion, just daylight. Charlie Carbon has almost forgotten its existence after all those years buried deep underground.

She screws up her face against the unexpected glare and peers out through half-opened eyes. The bright light is painful. It reaches the innermost part of her brain and energises her neutrons and protons. Suddenly she is wide awake and alert.

She gazes out in surprise. What magnificent colours! Much brighter than she can ever remember. It is quite overwhelming. Luscious greens, bright yellows, vivid pinks, cool blues. Charlie sits bolt upright and bathes in the light, soaking up its energy. Smiling, she chuckles,

"How beautiful! It's amazing!"

Gradually, as the hours tick by, the colours deepen and take on a golden glow. The sky darkens against the setting sun and Charlie Carbon begins to feel cold and tired again. The day has been exhausting.

Shivering slightly, Charlie squeezes herself into one of the crevices on her piece of coal to try and keep warm. She yawns loudly and within a few seconds the pile of coal begins to vibrate with the sound of ... yes, you've guessed it...

Ugggggggggh, phewwwwwwwww. Ugggggggggh, phewwwwwww!

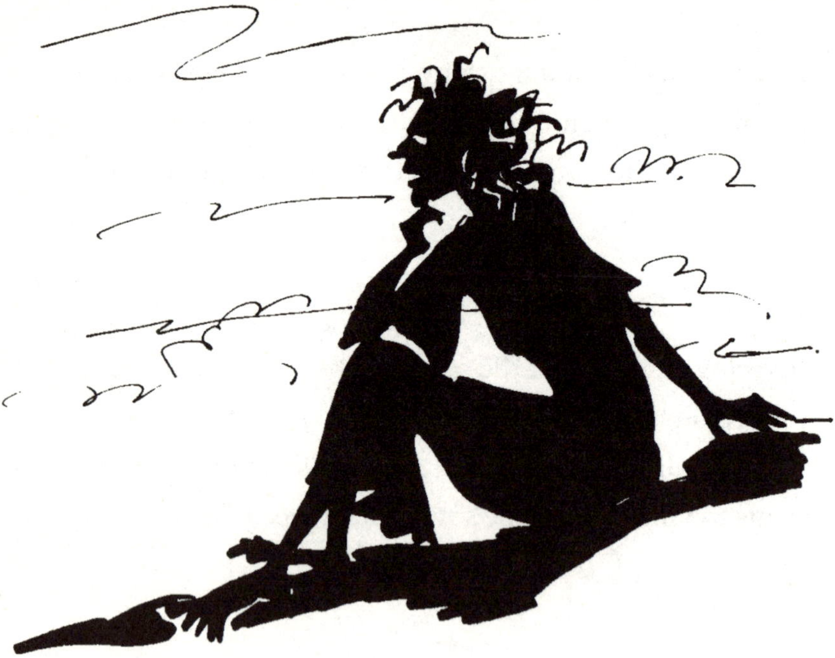

Something is pulling at her hair. Charlie Carbon wakes up with a start and grumpily complains, "What's that? My hair is caught. Ouch!"

Without opening her eyes, she changes her position, but the pulling continues.

"Oh, stop it, I'm trying to sleep."

She yawns loudly, adding, "Haven't had a good sleep for ages."

A shrill voice giggles and she feels her hair being pulled again.

"Sleepy Charlie Carbon!" teases the voice. "Sleepy Charlie Carbon!"

"Oh stop it," says Charlie in an irritated voice. "Just leave me alone can't you? Whoever you are. You're disturbing my electrons!"

"Can't catch me! Come on, you old thing, wake up. You've slept long enough."

"Go away, let me sleep!" grumbles Charlie, too tired to react to the "old thing".

But the pulling continues.

"Come on Charlie, you must remember me – Olive. You know, Olive Oxygen. We were friends way back in the past. We had a great time together, surely you remember!"

"Oh no," groans Charlie, "not you!"

"Come on, wake up. We had such fun together. You, me and my cousin Ophelia. She's here too!"

"Hiya, Charlie!" Ophelia Oxygen is holding hands with her cousin and bobbing up and down in the air excitedly. "Open your eyes, this is me, Ophelia. Don't you remember, we formed a gang."

"Yeah," interrupts Olive. "They called us the CO_2 gang – short for carbon dioxide, after you, me and Ophelia. You the carbon, and us two the oxygens."

"You must remember," adds Ophelia, "we had a smashing time. Come on, wake up and play again."

"Oh, no!" groans Charlie as she begins to remember.

"We had lots of fun," continues Olive Oxygen. "Dancing about together in the clouds. It was cool! Come on, old thing, let's do it again! We might even become a pop group. You never know!"

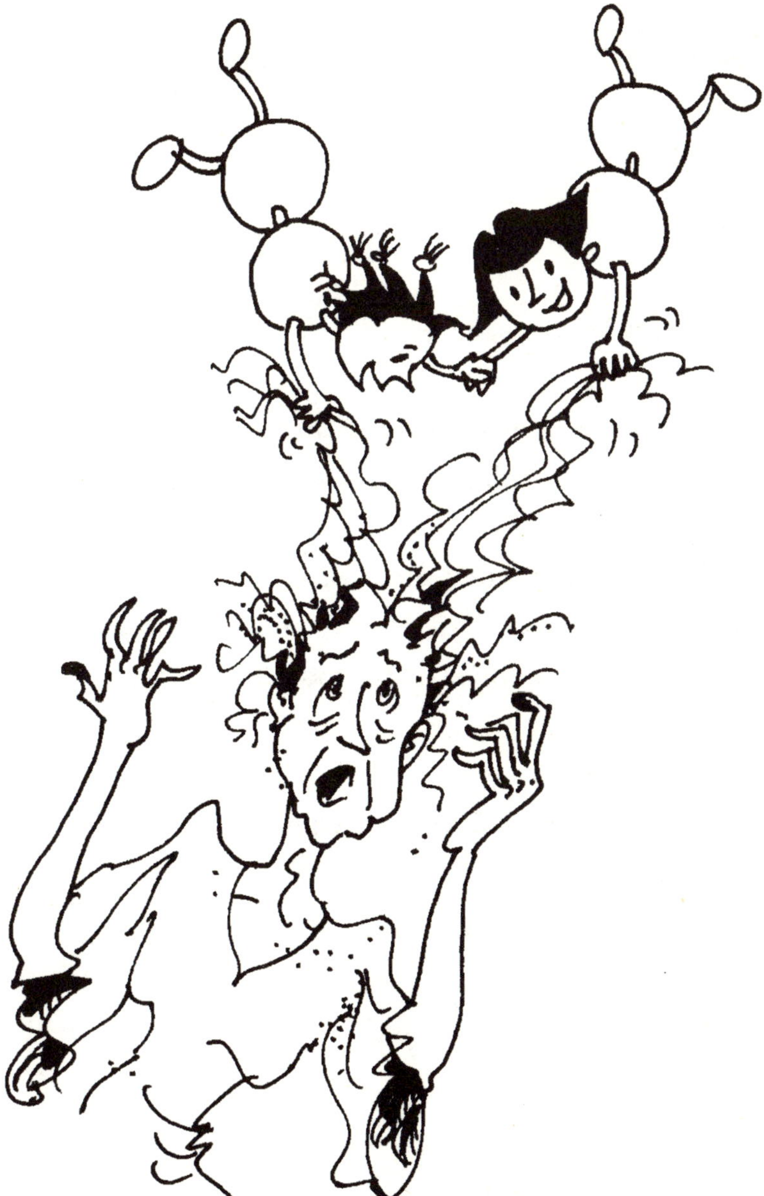

Charlie slowly opens one eye.

Olive looks much the same, bouncing about with her cousin Ophelia, as full of energy as ever.

"Oh do go away and find someone else to play with," Charlie says irritably. "I'm much too tired to bother with you. Anyway," she shivers, "I'm too cold to play! Its freezing here!"

"Not for long!" giggle Olive and Ophelia together. "Just you wait and see."

There is a sudden scraping sound and gradually, before Charlie realises what is happening, the world becomes full of lovely colours again – warm oranges, soft yellows and glowing reds.

Charlie looks round and sees that she is in a dark room and everything in the room is beginning to spring into life. The room sways this way and that as she looks through flickering flames.

The piece of coal with Charlie clinging to its surface is placed on a fire. Charlie has no idea how she got there, but here she is, on a fire. She must have slept through most of the journey.

And now the fire is alight. At last, she is beginning to feel deliciously warm.

"Uhmmmmmm," murmurs Charlie. "This is more like it. My old bones are warming through." Gradually the flames begin to lick around Charlie's piece of coal and it begins to get even hotter.

"Hey, I say, that's enough, I'm warm enough now. I don't need it to be any hotter than this."

But the fire doesn't stop. In fact the flames get so close that one brushes against a few strands of Charlie's hair. There is a sizzling sound and an awful smell of burning cheese.

"Oh no, no more heat please! This is enough. I'm too hot and my hair is getting singed. Olive, where are you? Can't you help me?"

"Here," says a voice, "I'm here. What do you want? I thought you wanted to be left alone."

"Oh, I do, er, no, I mean I don't. It's just getting too hot. I can't stand it. Oh Olive, help me, can't you? And you too Ophelia."

"Oh, so you're changing your tune now are you?" teases Olive. "You want to come and play after all."

"Oh no. I mean, yes. Yes, I do want to play. Just help me, please," she wails. 'Help me, I'm beginning to burn!"

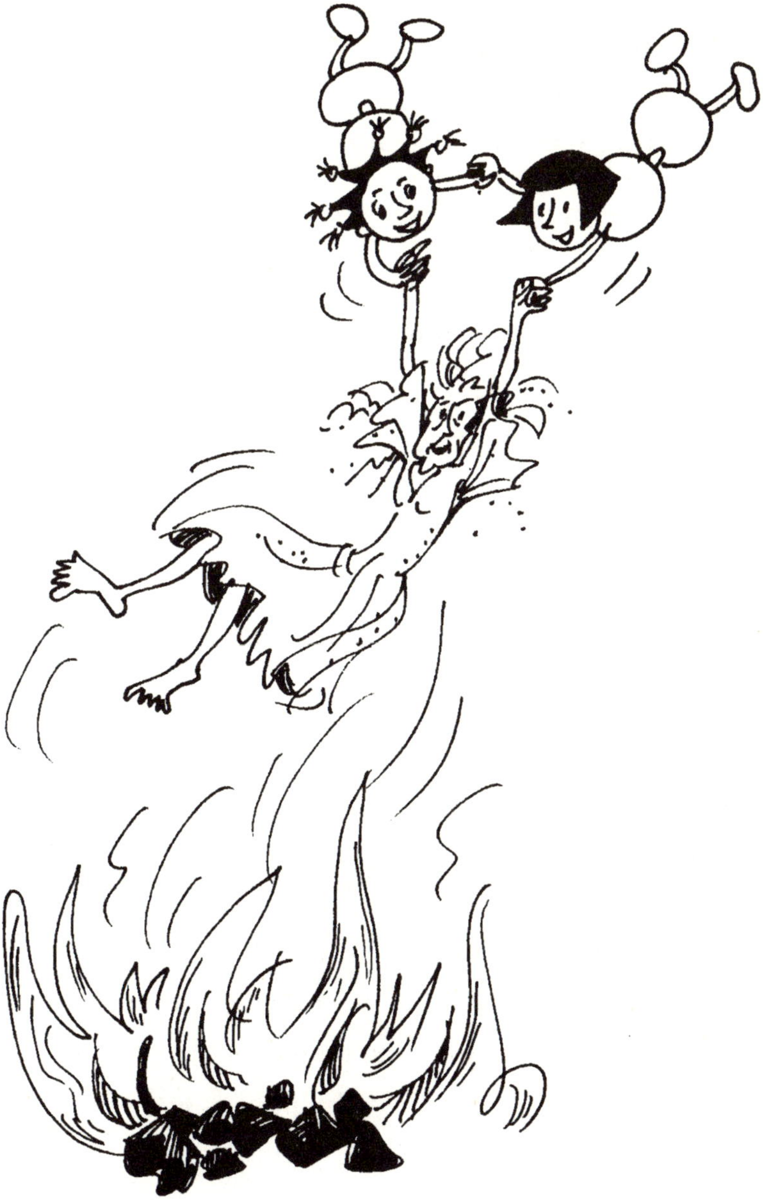

"OK," say the cousins together. "Just stretch out your arms and we'll pull. One, two, three, puuuuuuullllllll!" The cousins each grab an arm and pull and pull and pull until suddenly,

WHOOOOOOOOSH!

Charlie Carbon is free from the heat of the flames. But before she can say 'thank you', Olive giggles. "Hee hee, now we've got you. Now you'll have to play because you're joined to us. We're all joined together again."

"Yep," adds Ophelia, "we're a molecule once more. A molecule of carbon dioxide. Great – this'll be fun! It's the carbon dioxide gang again, watch out everyone, here we come!"

Charlie's "Oh no!" is lost as she finds herself rapidly speeding upwards, high into the room and out through a crack where the windows don't quite meet.

The cousins bounce about, dragging the old lady behind them. Up in the clouds, in and out of the houses, hovering above rivers and high above the cities. Poor Charlie is feeling very tired and longing for the peace and quiet of her lump of coal underground.

"When can we stop?"

"Oh, not yet, not for a while, we're having such fun…" Olive's words trail away as they are caught in gust of wind.

"Come on, old thing, let's explore over there."

"Oh no," wails Charlie. "It's OK for you two, but I'm not young any more. I need a rest."

They bounce around for days, weeks and years until, finally, one day our molecule of carbon dioxide lands on a new, pale-green leaf on a huge beech tree. The leaf is covered with a downy mass of fine hairs and feels soft and comfortable.

"Oh this is bliss!" sighs Charlie. "At last we can stop for a while and I can have a sleep."

They settle down on the leaf, but before they know what is happening they get sucked into one of the tiny holes on its surface. They are now in a wonderful, green, exciting world full of minute tubes and passages turning this way and that. As they are sucked deeper and deeper into the flesh of the leaf, it grows darker and cooler. Charlie manages to persuade Olive and Ophelia to settle down with her in a tiny cell at the end of one of the passages. It's rather like being back underground.

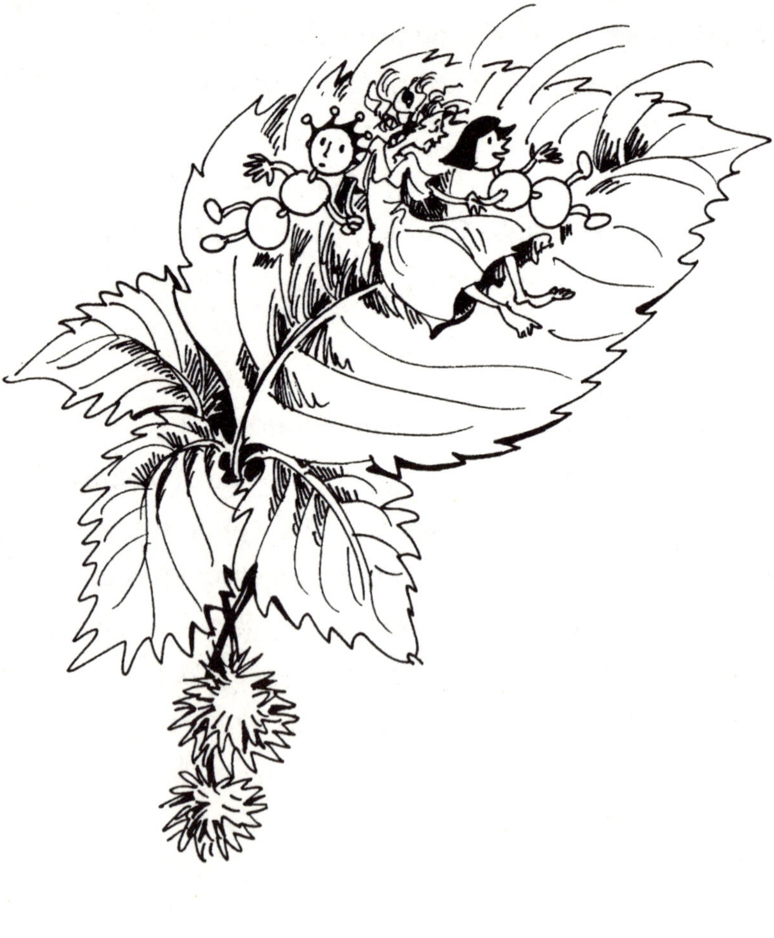

Charlie Carbon falls asleep. She sleeps and sleeps.

Uggggggggh, phewwwwwwww. Uggggggggh, phewwwwwww!

Eventually, Olive and Ophelia get bored waiting for her to wake up and bounce back along the passages into the open air.

But Charlie Carbon sleeps on, month after month, year after year. She becomes part of the tree, joined to other atoms. But Charlie is too tired to even bother to acknowledge their existence. She snoozes away contentedly, lost in her dreams.

The snows come and go, the rain lashes, the sun shines and the winds blow. And still Charlie Carbon sleeps on.

Eventually, after a few hundred years, the beech tree dies and becomes buried under layers of mud. Slowly, slowly changes happen. So slowly that Charlie can't remember just how it all occurs.

Million of years pass to a time in the future when human beings are no longer around.

The remains of the beautiful beech tree are crushed and squeezed, compacted and compressed together till they became so hard and dense that they change into coal. Shiny, rich black lumps of coal. And still Charlie Carbon sleeps on.

Uggggggggggh, phewwwwwwwww. Uggggggggggh, phewwwwwww.

One day, Charlie wakes up briefly, just for a few minutes. She peers out of half-closed eyes to see that she is back underground again, curled up tightly in a small crevice on a piece of coal. It is warm, dark and peaceful. For a second, a picture flashes into her mind of being pulled around in the clouds by two young boisterous atoms, back and forth, up and down and swirling round and round. But no sooner does she focus on the image than it fades away. It must have been a dream. Charlie Carbon yawns, smiles contentedly and settles back down to sleep.

Uggggggggh, phewwwwwwww. Uggggggggh, phewwwwwww.

The **carbon cycle** has turned a full circle and Charlie Carbon is back where she began. Perhaps we'll have to wait another million years before her next adventure – who knows?

Uggggggggh, phewwwwwwww. Uggggggggh, phewwwwwww.

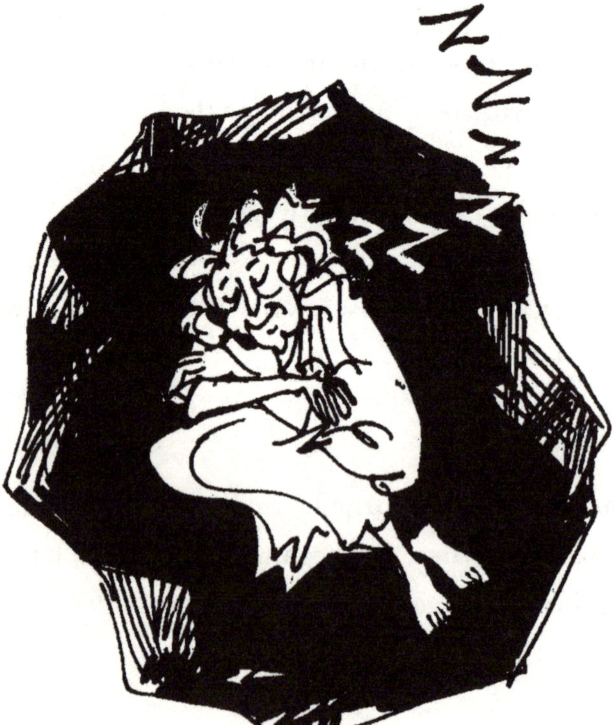

CARBON

- Carbon is a solid non-metal. When pure, it exists in one of two forms, either as graphite or diamond. Coal is an impure form of graphite.

- When coal is heated in air, it burns and the carbon joins with oxygen to form the colourless gas called carbon dioxide. As coal burns it gives out heat. Coal is therefore used as a fuel.

- Carbon is a very important element as it is present in the majority of the compounds which make up living things. Plants take in carbon dioxide and water and use energy from the sun to change them into sugars. In this process, called photosynthesis, oxygen is released into the air.

- The sugars are used by the plant to produce the energy which is needed for it to grow. During respiration, the sugars are burnt using oxygen from the air. Energy is released and water and carbon dioxide are formed as waste products. The carbon dioxide returns to the air.

- When plants die, they often become buried underground. Sometimes they decay and release carbon dioxide. In other cases, if the conditions are right, they change into coal after millions of years.

- These reactions form part of a cycle known as the *carbon cycle*.

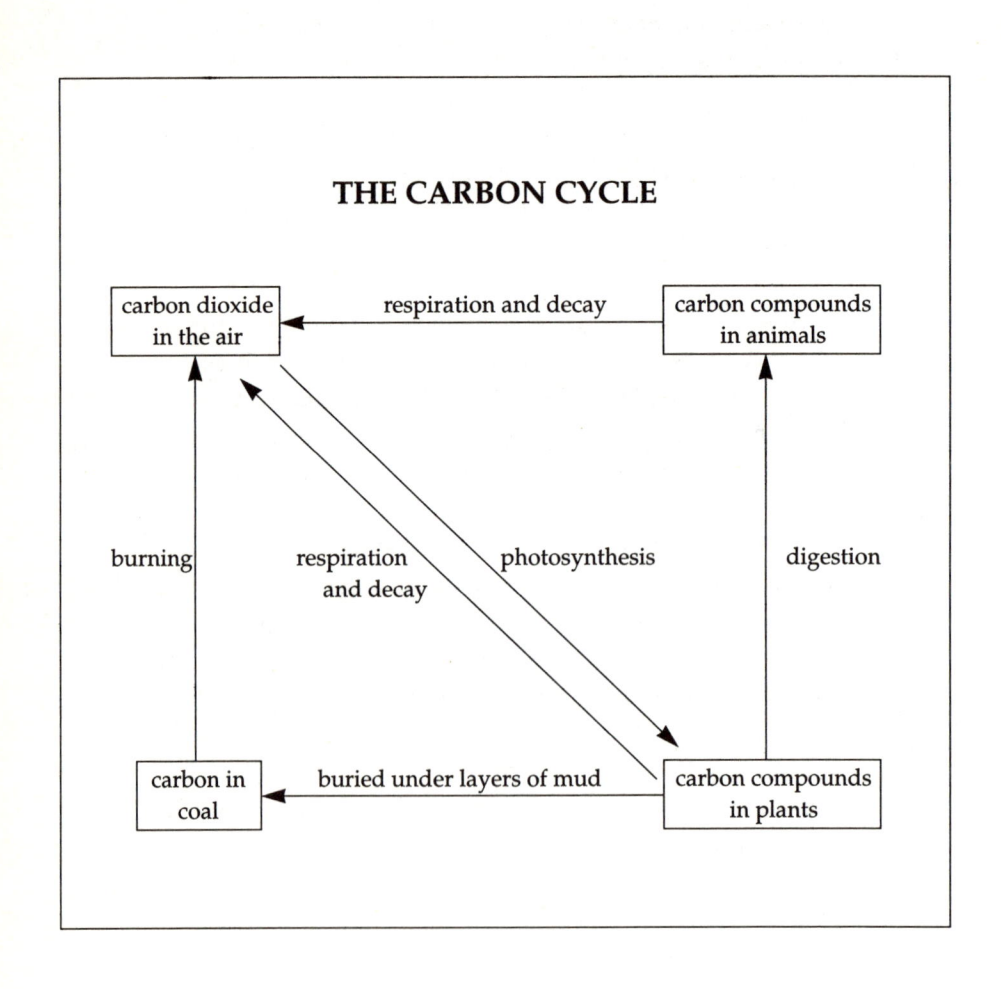

THE CARBON CYCLE

```
carbon dioxide  ←── respiration and decay ───  carbon compounds
   in the air                                     in animals
       ↑  ↑↓                                          ↑
       │                                              │
   burning   respiration    photosynthesis        digestion
             and decay
       │                                              │
   carbon in   ←── buried under layers of mud ──  carbon compounds
     coal                                           in plants
```

Sir Marcus Mercury

Sir Marcus Mercury took in a deep breath, puffed out his chest with pride and studied his gleaming image in the mirror.

"Oh," he murmured admiringly to his reflection, "what a picture! You **do** look good today."

His satin waistcoat was fastened with silver buttons. It was a tight fit and only just reached round his huge chest. His trousers were held up with silver braces as his waist had disappeared long ago. He put on his top hat, adjusted his blue bow tie with its silver dots and picked up his ornate silver walking stick. With another admiring glance at his reflection he added, "And I'm unique too! There's no other metal quite like me. Only I can roll around as a liquid – none of the others can do that." He sighed contentedly. "Oh, it's so good to be me!"

With that, he folded his copy of the *Daily Atomic News* under his arm and set off for work.

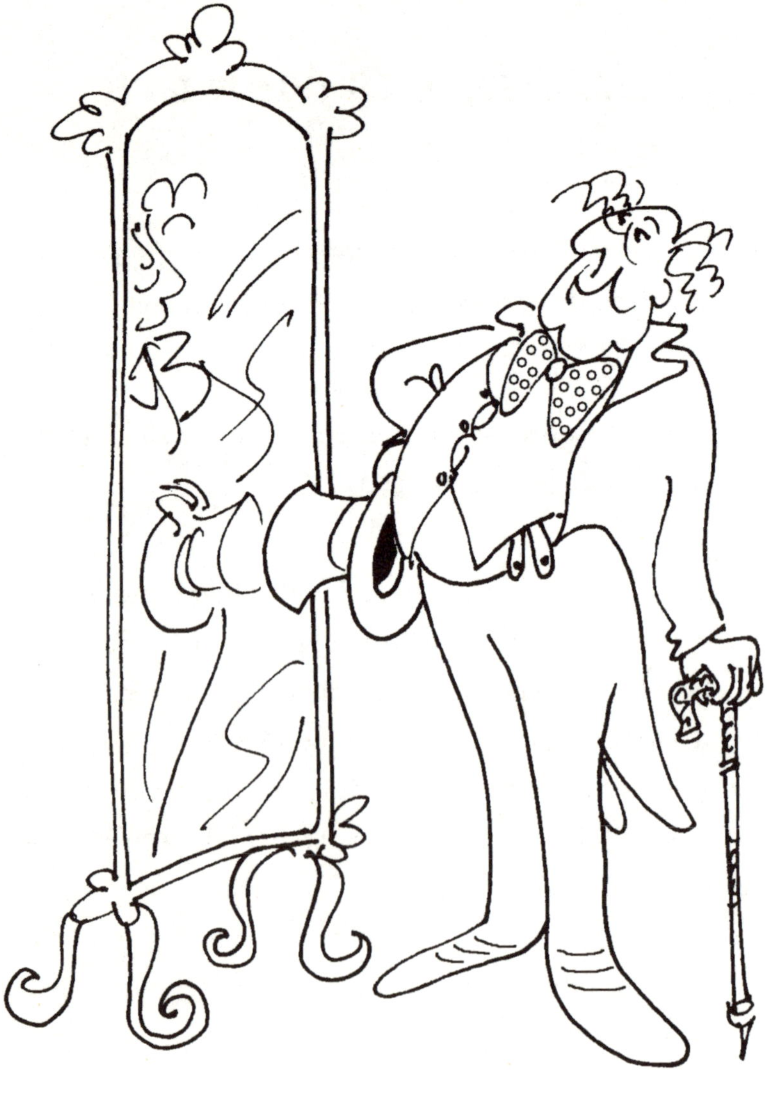

Work was in the Royal Atomic Hospital, an important building where most of the research on the health of atoms took place. And, to hear Sir Marcus Mercury talk, you'd think he was the most important person there. He just knew that without him the place couldn't function at all.

Today was Monday, and on Monday mornings he accompanied Sister or, as he described it, **she** accompanied **him**, on her visit to the patients in the wards. But before this, there were a few preparations to make. He rolled majestically along the corridor to the equipment room.

"Out of the way !" he snapped at Catherine Chlorine. "Move yourself, come on, quickly, there's work to be done."

Catherine Chlorine had not had a good morning. Her job entailed swimming around in a dish of water, chasing out the bugs and germs. But no sooner had she got rid of some of them, than more would appear as if from nowhere. They just kept multiplying, bugs of all shapes and sizes. Big fat green ones clinging to the glass surface, and slim worm-like pink ones darting this way and that through the water. It was exhausting work.

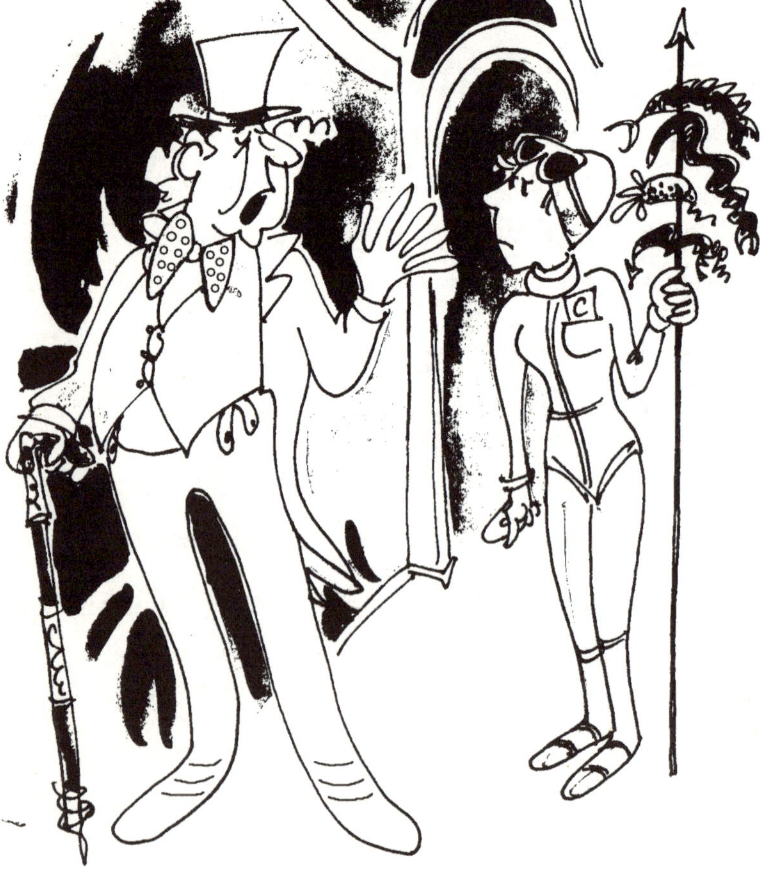
C

"Huh! You've not done very well this morning, have you?" boomed Sir Marcus Mercury. "You know how important it is to keep things clean so I can do my work properly."

Catherine blushed to the roots of her electrons and hung her head with embarrassment.

"S-s-s-sorry. I'm ever so sorry, it won't happen again." She sped quickly off after another bug.

Sir Marcus Mercury took off his hat, propped his walking stick against the wall and heaved himself up to the top of a thin glass tube standing in the dish of water. Breathing in, he pulled himself up to his greatest height and began to slowly squeeze into the tube. As he squeezed he grew longer and longer, and thinner and thinner, till he became a shiny silver thread down the whole length of the tube.

He kept squeezing and squeezing until all of a sudden there was a loud PLOP as most of his body landed in the glass bubble at the bottom. Immediately, he took up its shape and settled down comfortably, filling the whole of the bubble and a small part of the tube. Vibrating slightly after his efforts, he waited for work to begin.

His work in the thermometer involved finding the temperature of sick patients. When they were feverish, Sir Marcus Mercury would swell with pride and push out his chest so that more of his body squeezed up the tube. He carried on expanding until he reached the mark on the glass wall corresponding to the patient's temperature. When the temperature was lower, he would get smaller by forcing his electrons closer together. Contracting in this way, he would slip back along the tube until he reached the mark showing the new temperature.

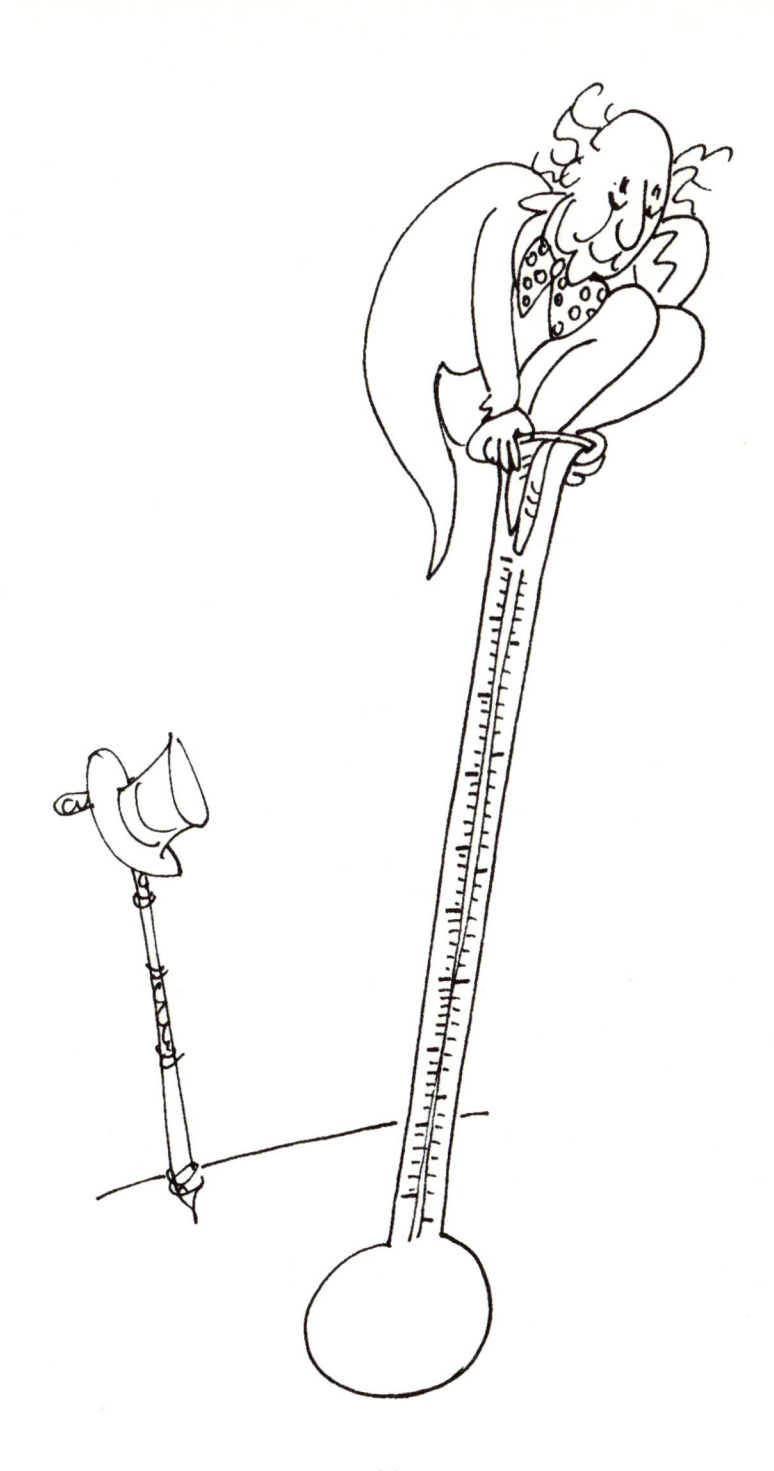

"Look at me everyone, I've almost reached the 40°C mark today! It takes a great deal of effort you know. I bet you all wish you could do this."

Charlie Carbon was dozing peacefully nearby, on the tip of a pencil. She gave a slight groan.

"There he goes again, showing off as usual."
She yawned. "He's unbearable, there's no peace any more."

"Yeah, I agree," whispered Olive Oxygen, who was hovering nearby with her cousin Ophelia. "It's the same every day – showing off, bossing us atoms about, finding fault. It's time someone taught him a lesson."

"Umm," agreed Charlie, "but don't ask me, I'm too tired, I need to sleep. You'll have to do it."

She yawned, settled back in her groove on the tip of the pencil, and fell asleep.

But Olive didn't need to be told. She was already hatching a plot.

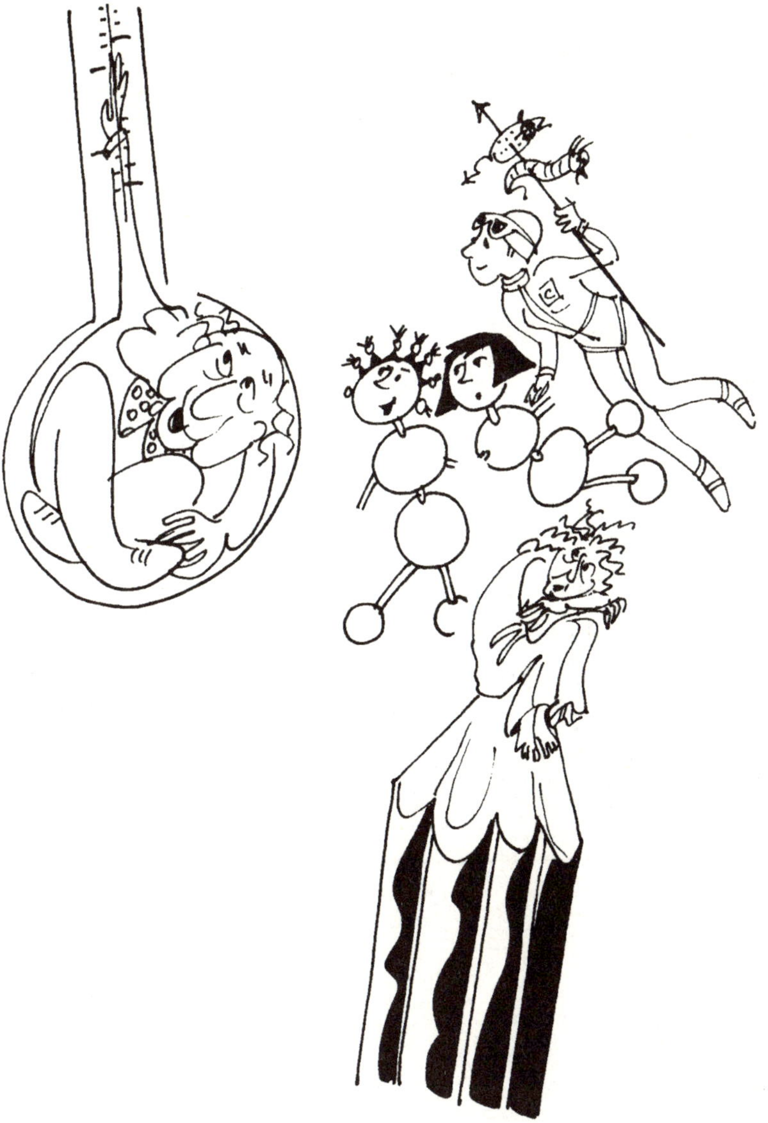

"Hey, Ophelia, I've an idea! This should bring Sir Marcus down an energy level or two – he's getting too big for his electrons. I'll need you to help as well."

The two atoms huddled together, merging their electrons. As the plan took shape, Olive and Ophelia started to bounce about excitedly in the air. But to put Olive's plan into action, they would have to wait till Tuesday, when Sir Marcus would be working in the dental laboratory, and at that moment Tuesday seemed a long way away.

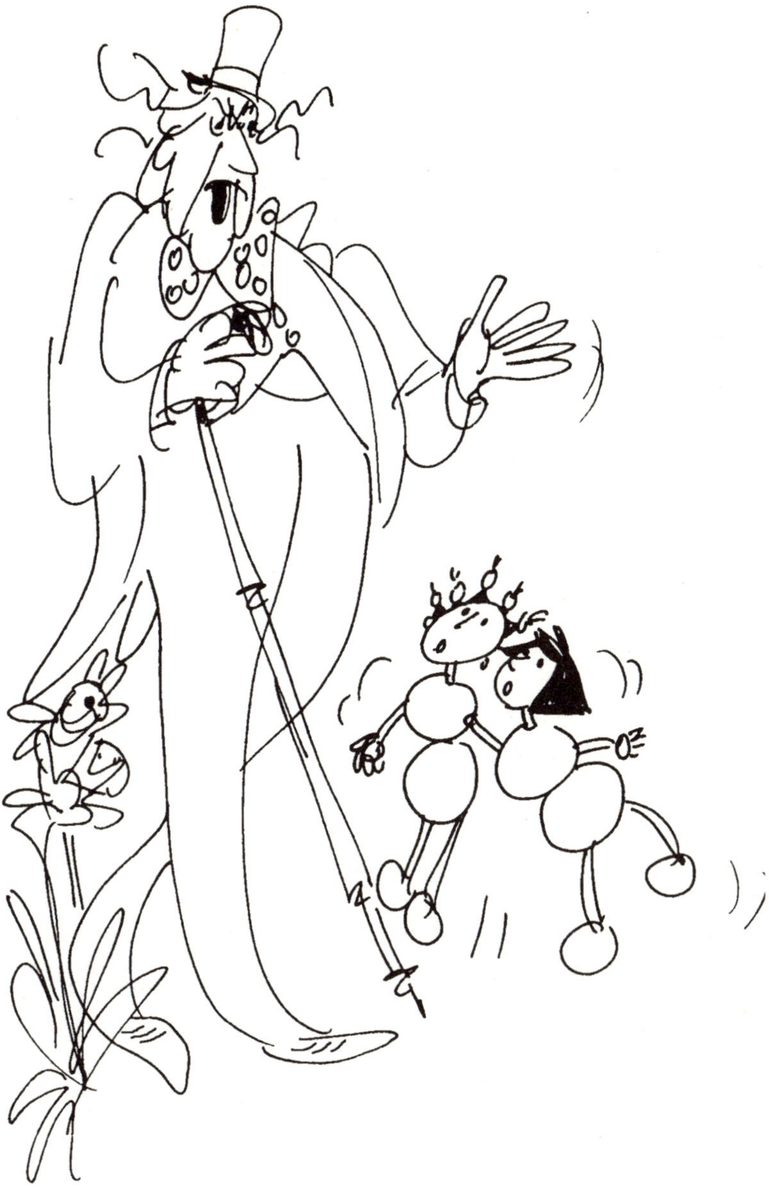

Tuesday afternoon was bright and sunny. Sir Marcus Mercury whistled contentedly, pleased with himself as he strutted, wobbled and rolled along the path to his afternoon shift in the hospital dental laboratory. He knew he looked wonderful.

"Out of my way!" he snapped at two young atoms playing electron marbles on the path.

They looked up and their mouths fell open in awe at the sight of what appeared to be a huge, wobbly, curved mirror advancing towards them. The daffodils reflected in his gleaming skin were distorted into frightening shapes and the reflection of the bright sun almost blinded them.

"Ohhhh, sorry."

They quickly bounced out of his way, hardly daring to breathe as he glided regally past.

Tuesdays involved working with Timothy Tin in the dental laboratory. Together, Sir Marcus Mercury and Timothy Tin made a special paste called an amalgam. This was used by the dentists to fill the holes in human's teeth. Everyone knew this work was important, but
Sir Marcus Mercury never stopped reminding them.

"How would humans manage to eat if it wasn't for me?"

He grudgingly admitted that Timothy Tin did have a **small** part to play, but it was he, Sir Marcus Mercury, who made the amalgam runny. Without him, the filling could never be squashed into the hole before setting to a hard solid. No more apples or chewy sweets if it wasn't for him!

That morning everyone was there on time, even Caspar Calcium, who usually overslept. Timothy Tin, Catherine Chlorine and Charlie Carbon (dozing on a lump of charcoal) were waiting with, of course, the Oxygen cousins bouncing about together in the air above. They were all in on the plan to teach Sir Marcus Mercury a lesson and were waiting excitedly for the fun to begin.

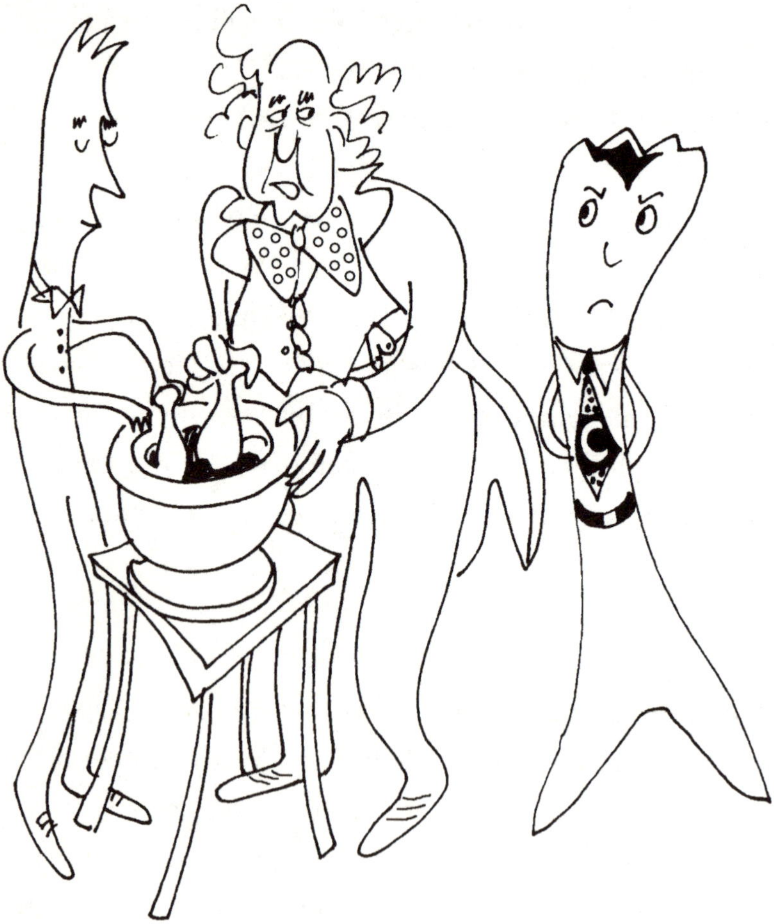

"I see you've done a bad job as usual Caspar," said Marcus scathingly as he peered at the hole in the decayed tooth. "It's about time you took your work more seriously. Too much social life."

Normally Caspar would have protested that it wasn't his fault at all, that he was fighting a losing battle when people ate loads of sweets and never cleaned their teeth. But today he just listened, because he knew that before long Sir Marcus Mercury would be eating his words.

"Come on, what are you lot staring at? There's work to be done. No time to stand around talking. Get moving."

Sir Marcus could never understand why they had to be told all the time and didn't just get on with things.

Now it was Olive's chance. Step one of her plan.

She sidled up to Sir Marcus Mercury, dragging Ophelia along with her, and gazed admiringly at him.

"Oh, Sir Marcus," she oozed, "how wonderful you look today! That tie really suits you."

"Oh, do you think so? Ummm, I like it too, seems to go with my skin colouring."

Ophelia nodded vigorously in agreement. It was her turn now.

"Yes, and I love to watch you working. No one else can swell up like you do in a thermometer. It's amazing. Just how do you manage to do it?"

"Mmm," agreed Catherine Chlorine, getting caught up in the game, "it's incredible. *Do* tell us how."

"Oh, you know, it's simple really." Sir Marcus Mercury had grabbed hold of the bait. "All I have to do is just expand a bit in the heat. Anyone could do it if they tried. Well, not everyone, you have to be a bit special and able to concentrate really hard. Of course, as you all know, I've had a lot of practice. That's why I'm so good at it."

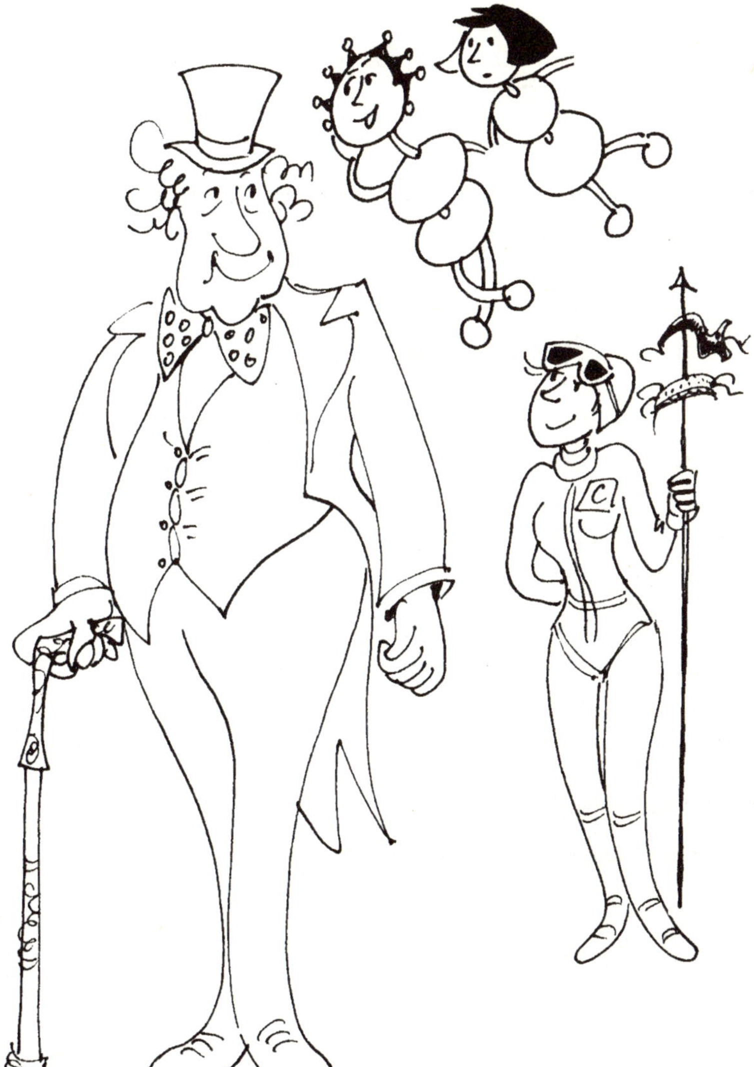

He paused for breath and Olive Oxygen immediately seized the opportunity.

"Oh, do show us, Sir Marcus, we'd love to see it again."

"Oh," he replied, somewhat taken aback. "I would do but, er, there's no heat."

"Oh, yes there is," said Olive, "there's a small fire over there – Charlie Carbon has just woken up long enough to make it nice and hot for you."

"Oh! Very well, if you *really* insist."

Sir Marcus pretended he needed a lot of persuasion, but he was actually delighted to show off his skills.

Sir Marcus Mercury rolled over the edge of a small dish above the fire and landed with a PLOP in the bottom. As the other atoms gathered round to watch, he began to swell with pride.

"You see! This is what I do. I'm getting bigger with the heat. Bigger and bigger. Simple really, once you know how of course. But it takes a lot of training."

"Oh, yes," murmured Olive and Ophelia together, "it's incredible how you do it!"

"Oh, can't you get bigger still?" encouraged Caspar Calcium, joining in with the fun. "Come on, Charlie," he added, "try a bit harder and get even hotter."

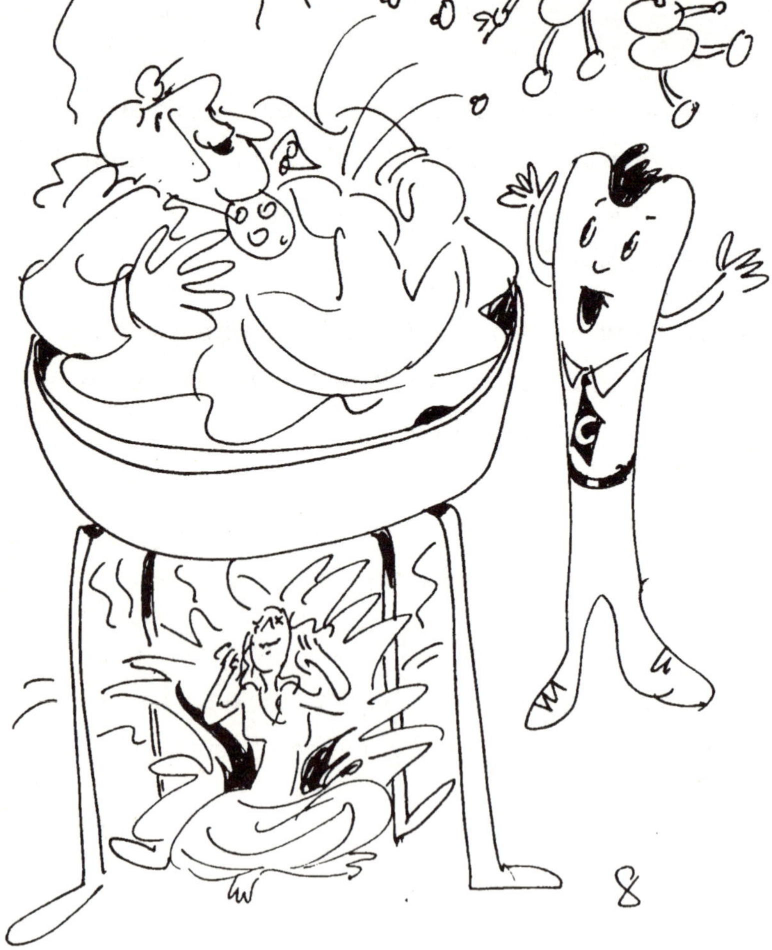

Charlie Carbon glowed redder and redder and Sir Marcus Mercury grew bigger and bigger.

Suddenly, **pop! pop! pop! pop! pop!** One by one all of the silver buttons on his waistcoat flew off with the strain. Ophelia caught one and slipped it into her pocket.

"More, more!" shouted Timothy Tin and Catherine Chlorine together, excitedly hopping from foot to foot. "Come on Charlie, you're doing well!"

Charlie puffed and panted and the fire grew hotter and hotter.

All of a sudden, Sir Marcus Mercury looked at his hands and shrieked with panic.

"What's happening? Just look at my skin – it's changing colour! Where's my silver sheen gone?"

Yes, his skin really was changing. The shiny, silver surface was becoming coated with a dull red powder. Frantically, Sir Marcus tried to rub it off, but no sooner had he exposed the shiny silver underneath than it too turned into the dull red powder.

"Oh, I can't stop it. My electrons are out of control. Help me, someone, help me can't you?"

Sir Marcus was frightened. He'd never experienced anything like this before. He cried out loudly as his huge silver form began to collapse into a heap of red dust. Gone was his pride and overbearing self-importance as he gradually turned into a pathetic pile of red powder in the bottom of the dish.

"Oh Olive, please help me! It's much too hot. Just grab my hands and pull me out. Quickly, please!"

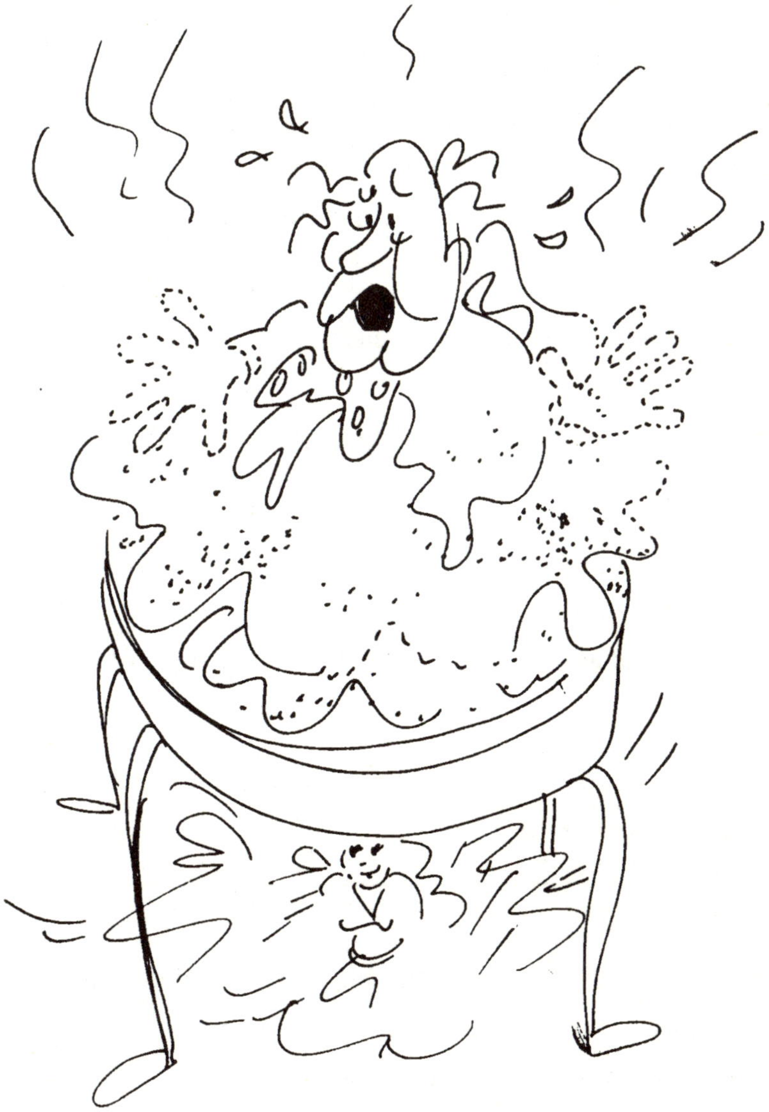

This was the moment Olive had been waiting for.
She let go of Ophelia and reached out for Sir Marcus, grabbing his arms tightly and holding on. As their electrons merged together they formed a new compound – the bright-red powder we call mercury oxide.

"Oh dear," sighed Sir Marcus, "where has my lovely body with its bright silver sheen gone?"

All the atoms around were laughing at his plight and he suddenly realised what had happened.

"You've trapped me, haven't you, Olive? You planned this to happen, didn't you? That's typical of you all. Why?" he asked indignantly. "It's not fair! I've never done anything to you."

There was a silence, broken only when Olive quietly asked, "Haven't you?"

Again there was a silence and Sir Marcus looked round hopefully at the circle of atoms gathered about the dish. But the faces were not at all friendly.

"Well, maybe I've been a bit difficult," he admitted grudgingly. "Only occasionally though, everyone has an off day or two. That's right isn't it?" No one replied.

"Well, maybe a bit more than occasionally. But you must help me, Olive, to get back to how I was."

Olive stared nonchalantly in front of her, pretending not to hear.

"Oh, **please**, Olive. All right, I'll try to be a bit more understanding in the future."

"Only try?" asked Olive.

"Oh well, all right then, I **will** be more understanding. How's that? And..." he took a deep breath and swallowed his pride, "I'm sorry for how I've been. Now help me, please?"

A murmur of surprise went round the circle. An apology from Sir Marcus Mercury! Whatever next?

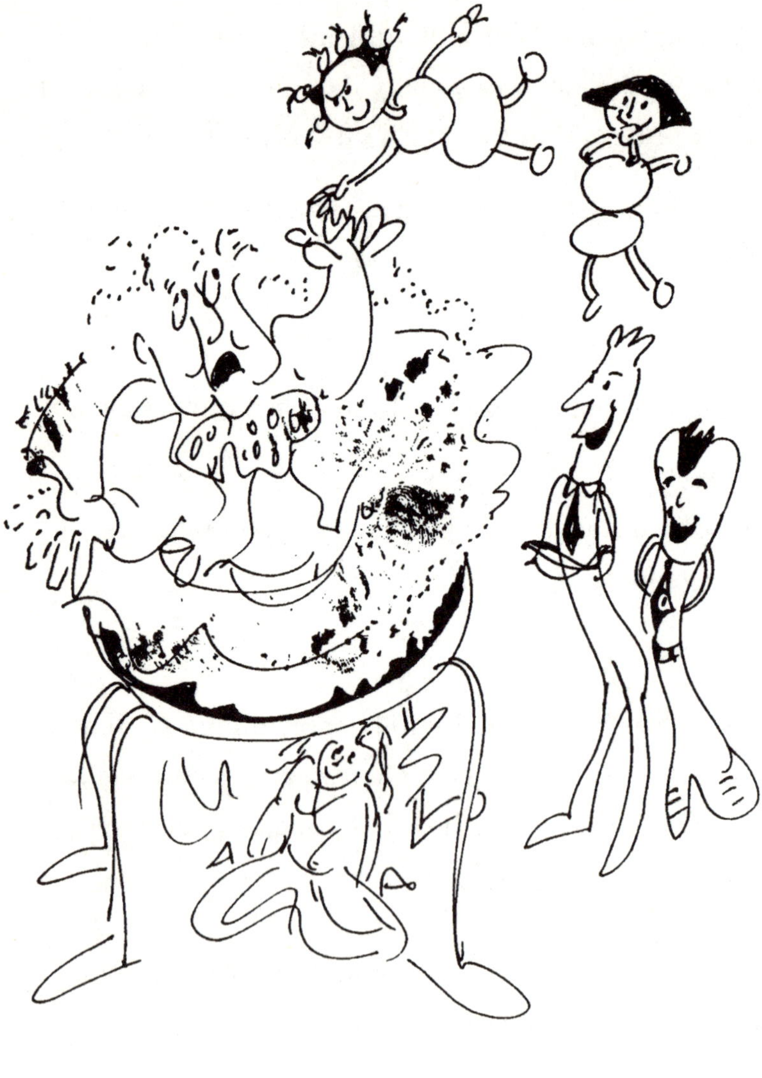

Before he had a chance to change his mind, Olive muttered, 'OK, we'll keep you to that." Then she clung onto him in the dish and asked Charlie Carbon to glow even more brightly.

Hotter and hotter. Olive and Marcus began to perspire.

Hotter and hotter. They began to vibrate and bounce about.

HOTTER and HOTTER. They moved more frantically until suddenly there was a long, loud, eeeeeeeeH! and they fell apart as separate atoms again.

Sir Marcus Mercury immediately resumed his original shape and colour. The only thing that had changed was the missing buttons from his waistcoat. Olive bounced away to join up with Ophelia who pinned one of the silver buttons like a badge of honour on Olive's dress. All the other atoms gathered round, grinning happily and patting Olive on the back.

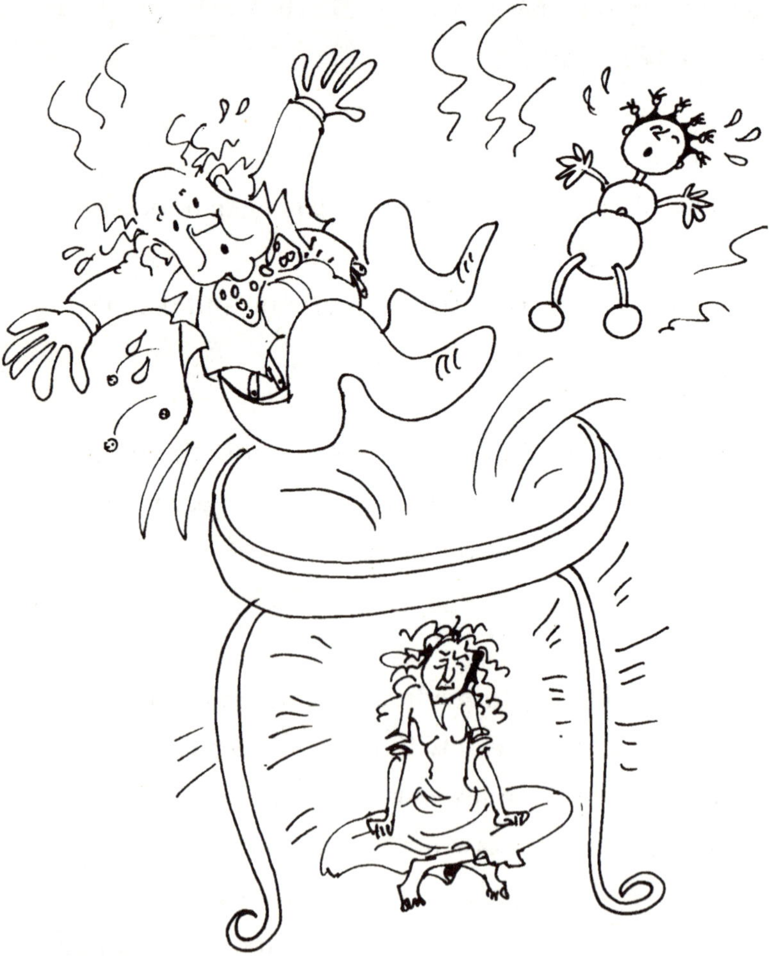

Sir Marcus Mercury slowly pulled himself out of the dish and painfully began to roll home. There would be no tooth-filling today. His clothes looked dishevelled and his head was not quite as high as usual.

But whether or not he really **did** behave differently – well, that's another story. After all, leopards don't often change their spots, do they?

MERCURY

- Mercury is a silver-grey metal which is a liquid at room temperature.

- When mercury is heated in air it combines with oxygen and forms a red compound called mercury oxide.
At a higher temperature, mercury oxide breaks down to form mercury and oxygen again.

- Mercury expands on heating and so is used in thermometers for recording temperatures.

- When mercury is mixed with tin, an alloy called **tin amalgam** is formed. This is used for dental fillings.

- Mercury is poisonous.